# Your rights and the law

Joshua Rozenberg and Nicola Watkins

J.M. Dent & Sons Ltd
London  Melbourne

First published 1986
© Joshua Rozenberg and Nicola Watkins 1986

This book is set in 10/12 Linotron Sabon by
Inforum Ltd, Portsmouth

Printed in Great Britain by
Cox and Wyman Ltd, Reading, for
J.M. Dent & Sons Ltd
Aldine House, 33 Welbeck Street, London W1M 8LX


British Library Cataloguing in Publication Data

Rozenberg, Joshua
    Your rights and the law.
    1. Civil rights—Great Britain
    I. Title   II. Watkins, Nicola
    344.102'85     JN906

    ISBN 0–460–02422–1

CB 33441 [3.95. 12.87]

# Contents

# Preface

This is a book about rights. In that sense it's a bit different from other potted guides to the law you may have seen in the bookshops. The first chapter is also rather unusual: it tells you a little about the rights you have, but there's a great deal more about what 'rights' really are. And the rest of the book, while outlining the rights different people have in different circumstances, is not afraid now and then to break off and tell you something strange or interesting about the law — even though it's not likely to find its way into a bald précis of the most basic facts.

So what you've got in your hands is a basic guide to many of the most important laws that apply in England and Wales. We've not tackled Scotland, Northern Ireland, or the other islands which make up the British Isles: their legal systems are of course different. But even so, we hope that people outside England and Wales will find something of interest in the pages that follow; much — though by no means all — of what we say applies throughout the United Kingdom and beyond.

In a rapidly changing world this book is as up-to-date as we can make it. It was completed late in 1985 but it takes full account of two major pieces of legislation which operate from 1986, the Police and Criminal Evidence Act and the Prosecution of Offences Act. We also look ahead to the Public Order Bill which is not likely to take effect much before 1987.

But here we must offer a word of warning. The law changes every day. No book — even the sophisticated loose-leaf variety that lawyers use — can ever be fully up-to-date. So you should check carefully whether there have been any changes to the laws that follow. And here's another warning. A little knowledge can be a dangerous thing, as John Pritchard says in the introduction to his own excellent guide to the law. All we can offer you is a little law on each of the topics we mention. There are always more details, fine print, exceptions and reservations. Those exceptions may affect you. And, needless to say, if you do find any errors, feel free to write and tell us. But in the meantime, since we are lawyers, we hope you will forgive us if we watch our backs: no responsibility for any loss occasioned to any person acting or refraining from action as a result of the material in this book can be accepted by the authors or publishers.

Chapters 1 to 3 were first drafted by Joshua Rozenberg; Chapters 4 to 8 by Nicola Watkins. Our thanks go to David Pannick, a barrister, Fellow of All Souls, and prolific writer on legal affairs, and to Stephen Gold, a solicitor and columnist in the *New Law Journal*, for reading the manuscript; to June Williams for her help on Legal Aid; to John Garey for his valiant attempts to do what the man on the Clapham omnibus is renowned for; and to many other friends in the legal profession for their advice and encouragement; any errors that remain are of course our own. Annette Kingham typed the book skilfully and with calm efficiency. We must also thank our respective employers for allowing us to take on this project; any opinions you may find hidden away in the pages that follow are of course ours and not those of the BBC (which has no opinions) or The Law Society (which has plenty).

Joshua Rozenberg

Nicola Watkins

# 1 *All rights*

Rights are wonderful things to have. We've all got them in a free society, though we may not know exactly what they are. Some of us have more rights than others; from time to time we're given new rights, and sometimes they're taken away from us. But what is a right? Where does it come from? And what rights do we have? These are questions we'll be dealing with in the pages that follow.

They're questions that are easier to ask than to answer. To understand why, you have to know how our legal system was designed. Or rather was not designed, because as most books on the British Constitution tell you somewhere around the second paragraph, we haven't got one, at least not a written constitution like everyone else has, even countries like the United States which have taken on the common law of England. We in Britain don't even have a modern Bill of Rights, or a criminal code.

## THE BRITISH CONSTITUTION

The lawyers will tell you that of course we've got a constitution, and a fine one at that; it's just a little hard to find because nobody's got around to writing it down. That, they say, doesn't make it inferior to the written constitutions of the United States, or of our partners in Europe, or of the Commonwealth countries to which we've given independence. Indeed, says the argument, constitutional conventions can offer greater protection than grandiloquent documents.

It was Dicey who first wrote about 'the conventions of the constitution' in his book on constitutional law published a hundred years ago, *Introduction to the Study of the Law of the Constitution* (1885). His examples were all about Parliament:

\* The sovereign must assent to any bill passed by the two houses of Parliament.

\* The House of Lords does not originate any money bill.

\* When the House of Lords acts as a court of appeal, no peer who is not a law lord takes part in the decisions of the house.

\* Ministers resign office when they have ceased to command the confidence of the House of Commons.

\* A bill must be read a certain number of times before passing through the House of Commons.

None of these is a law as such (although now there are statutory restrictions on what the Lords can do with a money bill). All these conventions, however, are so fundamental to our constitution that they have survived quite happily through the hundred years since Dicey listed them.

But the constitution does change. There was apparently once a convention that the Home Secretary should be present at a royal birth; and there are now many more conventions than when Dicey was writing. Indeed the whole complicated system of cabinet government depends on these conventions, as does the work of Parliament. Take the Prime Minister, for example. We've had one since early in the eighteenth century, but not because Parliament sat down one afternoon and passed a law saying so. Indeed it wasn't until 1917 that a statute first noticed we had such a person, when the official 'now popularly known as Prime Minister' was allowed to live at Chequers. By that reckoning the cabinet was first spotted in 1937 when Parliament decided cabinet ministers would get salaries; likewise the Leader of the Opposition. The Ministers of the Crown Act 1937 did mention in passing that there were such things as political parties, but it wasn't until 1969 that MPs came out of the closet and allowed party names to be printed on ballot papers.

As Sir Ivor Jennings wrote in *The Law and the Constitution*, these Acts didn't validate or legalise the conventions; they simply recognised that they exist. The strength of the conventions lies in the fact that they're accepted; anyone who defies them knows that in the last resort Parliament can make them into a more visible kind of law.

Enough then on constitutional conventions, but you see how difficult it is to draw up a list of rights when even the most basic constitutional structure isn't written down anywhere. How much easier it would be, runs the argument, if all our rights were gathered together in one pre-packed, courtroom-ready, Act of Parliament. Let's call it a Bill of Rights. Unfortunately it doesn't exist. At least, not in the form of a modern Act of Parliament.

## Human rights: Europe

What we do have is the European Convention for the Protection of Human Rights and Fundamental Freedoms, adopted by the Council of Europe in 1950. The Convention includes most (though not all) of the human rights which two years earlier the United Nations adopted in its Universal Declaration on Human Rights. But the Council of Europe went further than the United Nations in providing for the first time a way of enforcing those rights – even against reluctant governments.

The European Convention – which took effect in September 1953 – protects rights of a civil and political nature. The main ones are:

* The right to life.
* The right to liberty.
* The right to a fair trial.
* Respect for private and family life, home and correspondence.
* Freedom of thought, conscience and religion.
* Free speech.
* Freedom of peaceful assembly, including the right to join a trade union.
* The right to marry and start a family.

11

The Convention and its amendments prohibit:

* Torture.
* Slavery.
* Retrospective criminal laws.
* Discrimination in allowing rights under the Convention.

There is quite a lot of small print, however, and the Convention recognises that some rights may be restricted on grounds of public safety, national security, the economic well-being of a country, public health and morals, the rights of others, and the prevention of crime. But there are no significant exceptions to the right to life, the ban on torture and the ban on the retroactivity of the criminal law.

There are 21 countries in the Council of Europe and they have all ratified the Convention (Britain was the first). In four of them – Cyprus, Greece, Malta and Turkey – only the government is allowed to bring proceedings against the government of another state in the Council. An example was the case brought in 1971 by the Irish Republic against the United Kingdom over interrogation of terrorist suspects in Northern Ireland – so far the only dispute between governments which got all the way up to the European Court of Human Rights. But then there have been fewer than 20 cases brought to the Court by states, compared with over ten thousand individual applications from the 17 countries which allow them.

And yet some of these 17 countries offer a lower level of protection to their citizens than others. Most of them offer a bonus – they include major countries like Austria, Belgium, France, Germany, Italy, the Netherlands and Spain. The ones without the bonus include the Scandinavian countries, Ireland, Liechtenstein, Malta – and the United Kingdom.

And the bonus? It's the right to enforce the Convention in the domestic courts, instead of having to take the long and difficult road to Strasbourg.

That road, incidentally, can be as long as nine years; even the shortest case which got as far as the Court took three years. And there was the utterly loony example in 1983 of a complaint against Switzerland that a delay of 3½ years in hearing a case before the Swiss courts contravened the provision in the Convention which requires 'a fair hearing within a reasonable time'; the European court agreed, but took more than 3½ years to reach its decision.

One reason for the delay is the complicated procedure involved. An individual begins by sending an application to the European Commission of Human Rights (address: Council of Europe, B.P.431 R6, F–67006 Strasbourg Cedex, France). Do not, by the way, confuse the European Commission in Strasbourg with the European Commission in Brussels; the Brussels one is part of the Common Market, and the Common Market is nothing to do with the Council of Europe. (The fact that the Common Market's European Parliament meets at Strasbourg in the Council of Europe building is simply a trap for the unwary.)

The Commission first has to decide whether a complaint is 'admissible', and it's at this stage that nine cases in ten will fall by the wayside. If the Commission can't bring about a 'friendly settlement' of an admissible case, it can refer it on to the European Court of Human Rights. Do not, by the way, confuse the European Court of Human Rights at Strasbourg with the European Court of Justice at Luxembourg; the Luxembourg one is part of the Common Market, and the Common Market is nothing to do with the Council of Europe. (The fact that the Common Market's European Parliament has its offices in Luxembourg is simply a trap for the unwary.) If the Court finds that the Convention has been broken, it can award damages and costs to a successful applicant. More important, governments are bound to comply with the judgments of the court which go against them. Compliance is supervised by the Council of Europe's Committee of Foreign Ministers: the ultimate sanction for disobeying the court could be expulsion from the Council.

But in practice governments eventually comply with the Court's rulings – up to a point. An example is the *Malone* decision in 1984 that telephone tapping in Britain was in breach of the article in the European Convention which says everyone has the

13

right to respect for his private and family life, his home and his correspondence. That led to the Interception of Communications Act 1985, which allows the Home Secretary to issue warrants allowing communications to be intercepted if he thinks it's necessary in the interests of national security; to prevent or detect serious crime; or to safeguard the economic well-being of the United Kingdom.

## Human Rights: Britain

The idea, though, of avoiding this long and difficult road to Strasbourg clearly has its attractions. Incorporating the Convention into our own domestic law would offer British citizens a speedy and effective remedy whenever their human rights are violated, and it would give British judges the power to interpret a convention which is effectively binding on the United Kingdom already. And so it was that distinguished judge Lord Scarman decided he would introduce his Bill of Rights as a Private Member's Bill in the House of Lords. Announcing his plans on the BBC Radio 4 programme *Law in Action* in February 1985, Lord Scarman said his bill would incorporate into English law those parts of the European Convention which set out the civil rights we mentioned earlier.

In making his announcement Lord Scarman said his bill would not restrict the powers of Parliament, or the government. 'It would compel the Executive to exercise its powers lawfully,' he said. 'It would compel the Executive to recognise and comply with rights which are already found in the English common law.'

It's extremely rare, if not unprecedented, for a serving judge to introduce legislation. But Lord Scarman's plans were not nearly as radical as those he proposed in his own Hamlyn lectures ten years earlier. Then he said there should be a new constitutional settlement: 'The legal system must now ensure that the law of the land will itself meet the exacting standards of human rights declared by international instruments, to which the United Kingdom is a party, as inviolable. This calls for entrenched or fundamental laws protected by a Bill of Rights – a constitutional law which it is the duty of the courts to protect even against the power of Parliament. In other words,' said Lord Scarman, 'there must be a constitutional restraint placed upon the legislative power which is designed to protect the individual citizen from instant legislation, conceived in fear or prejudice and enacted in breach of human rights.'

Lord Scarman's attempt to introduce a Bill of Rights is not the first. Over the past ten years there have been a number of attempts to give the European Convention 'the force of law', and to make it 'enforceable by action in the courts of the United Kingdom'. These proposals all say that the Convention is to prevail over existing laws if there's any conflict between the two. The Convention would also prevail over subsequent Acts of Parliament unless the new Act was clearly intended to overrule the Convention. There would also be a power to avoid having to comply with the Convention 'in time of war or other public emergency threatening the life of the nation'. None of these attempts to introduce a Bill of Rights made much parliamentary progress.

Lord Scarman's bill, when it was published in November 1985, looked a little different: it was called the Human Rights and Fundamental Freedoms Bill and is worth reading in some detail.

Strictly speaking, it wasn't Lord Scarman's bill at all: it was presented to Parliament by Lord Broxbourne, a former Conservative MP. But Lord Scarman was a driving force behind it, explaining that a Bill of Rights embodying the European Convention was 'needed to safeguard the individual'. He went on to explain that the courts needed its guidance 'to perform their checking and balancing function . . . to provide the citizen with an effective guard for his rights and freedoms'. Lord Scarman said that 'the legislature would look to it as a canon of just legislation'.

The bill begins by saying that the 'fundamental rights and freedoms' shall have the force of law in the United Kingdom. 'Fundamental rights and freedoms' means the rights and freedoms guaranteed by the European Convention on Human Rights. The next clause says that ministers and others holding public office must not infringe the fundamental rights and freedoms of anyone else in the United Kingdom. Anyone adversely affected by the infringement of fundamental rights and freedoms can sue (though there will normally be a time limit of six months in which to begin proceedings).

The next clause in the bill is crucial. It applies to all Acts of Parliament already in existence. These are in future to be reinterpreted. Any action allowed under existing legislation can be taken only in so far as it does not infringe anyone's fundamental rights and freedoms. This seems to mean that any legislation which is inconsistent with the European Convention is effectively repealed: all statutes must in future be read subject to the provisions of the Convention and where they disagree the Convention prevails.

The clause then goes on to deal with future legislation – legislation passed after the bill itself becomes law. Again, action can only be taken to the extent that it doesn't infringe fundamental rights and freedoms. But there's an exception: a future Act may exclude the Convention if Parliament so decides.

The bill then goes on to allow the judges to take account of the Convention, the additional protocols, and law reports of cases before the European Court of Human Rights and the European Commission of Human Rights.

At the end of the bill there's a let-out clause. If at any time the Queen declares by Order in Council that there exists a state of war or other public emergency threatening the life of the nation, she may take such measures as may appear to her to be strictly required by the exigencies of the situation – even if they abrogate fundamental rights and freedoms. But this emergency power is limited: there are some fundamental rights and freedoms which can never be taken away. These include the right to life under Article 2 of the European Convention (except in respect of 'death resulting from lawful acts of war'); the right not to be subjected to torture or to inhuman or degrading treatment or punishment; the right not to be held in slavery; and the right not to be charged with a crime which was not an offence at the time it was committed (this of course is the duty on governments not to pass retrospective criminal legislation – or even to increase penalties retrospectively).

The Queen must always act on the advice of her ministers (who – if they are in the cabinet – are members of the Council mentioned in the bill, the Privy Council). So an Order in Council, though made in the name of the Queen, is in reality little more than a decision of the cabinet. Nevertheless, the decision to make an Order in Council on a matter of this importance would – one hopes – not be taken lightly.

This then was Lord Scarman's bill – a brave attempt to strengthen the rights of British citizens by providing effective and accessible remedies in the courts of the United Kingdom for anyone who could show his or her rights had been infringed by a public authority. On its publication the bill had the support of politicians from all parties, and more than twenty voluntary organisations skilfully marshalled by the Rights Campaign (60 Chandos Place, London WC2N 4HG, telephone 01–240 1719).

But no bill can become law without government support – or at least government acquiescence – and it seemed far from likely at the time Lord Scarman's bill was published that such support would be readily forthcoming. And that can hardly come as much of a surprise to Lord Scarman and his many supporters. Ministers are unlikely to agree to anything that reduces their powers unless they really have to; indeed, some months earlier the Solicitor General, Sir Patrick Mayhew MP, was worried that giving the judges power to rule on difficult 'political' questions would make the political status of our judges much more of an issue. At the moment we in Britain manage to preserve the appearance that all our judges are politically neutral; in the sense that they don't wear party rosettes on polling day that's certainly true, but it is hard to avoid the impression that judges incline naturally and even subconsciously towards the Establishment (as Professor John Griffith argues with some force in *The Politics of the Judiciary*). The arguments on both sides are fully discussed by Michael Zander in the new (1985) edition of his pamphlet *A Bill of Rights?*

## A criminal code?

Once you've discovered that our civil rights in Britain aren't written down anywhere more authoritative than in a book like this, you won't be surprised to find that our criminal code doesn't yet exist either. At the moment if you want to know whether something's a criminal offence you have to study Acts of Parliament going back more than six hundred years, and the many thousands of cases which together make up the Common Law. A criminal code would replace all this law with just one Act, which would clearly be much easier to find and get hold of. Because it could use modern language it would also be easier to read; what's more, it would get rid of inconsistencies in the present law and lead to greater certainty. A report on codification of the criminal law was published by the Law Commission in March 1985; it contained the first attempt to codify the general principles of criminal liability for more than a hundred years. The Law Commission, which was set up by Parliament to promote reform of the law, has for many years believed the criminal law should be codified. It asked Professor John Smith of Nottingham University and a small team of academic lawyers to produce a draft code, and welcomed the result. It has asked for public discussion on whether a considerable amount of work and parliamentary time should go into a re-statement of the law that might not – in itself – make any major changes to the law.

Lord Scarman, who became the first chairman of the Law Commission in 1965, spoke about codification of English law in a lecture the following year. He wondered whether the 'quality of our judge-made law – its flexibility, its certainty, its capacity to develop in response to the stimuli of actual life conveyed through the channels of litigation to the minds of the judges – is such that its unmanageable bulk must be accepted'. In response to the question Lord Scarman pointed out that it was not the primary function of judges to legislate. Codification, he said, was both desirable and possible: in Roscoe Pound's words, an 'attempt to reshape the law by judicial overruling of leading cases is no substitute for well-drawn, comprehensive legislation'.

## Rights – and duties

All that was really by way of introduction to the questions posed in the first paragraph of this book. What then is a right?

One thing needs to be made very clear. Judges are fond of reminding people that they sit in courts of law, not courts of morals. This is a book of law, not a book of morals. And they're not the same thing. David Pannick, the barrister, was writing in the *Guardian* recently about David Waddington, the Home Office Minister responsible for immigration: 'Mr Waddington', he wrote, 'repeatedly fell over himself in his efforts to remove from the United Kingdom families who had every right, except a legal right, to remain here.'

### What is a legal right?

The branch of law dealing with abstract and theoretical questions of this sort is rather grandly called Jurisprudence. Even by legal standards it's a fairly slow-moving area, and thus it is that Sir John Salmond's textbook *Jurisprudence*, which he first published in 1902, is still read today. Turn then to his chapter on Rights, and at the top of the page you will see – boldly printed as the first sub-heading – Wrongs.

He's got a point of course. It's easy to see that a wrong is something that's against the law. Salmond then points out that everyone is under a 'duty' not to commit a wrong. And then he explains that if we, Rozenberg and Watkins, owe you a duty, you have a 'right' against us. So that's what a right is.

But if one person has a right, does it follow inevitably that someone else has a duty? Sir John Salmond believed every right must be a right against someone – and so that someone therefore owes a duty to the person with the right. It follows that there can't be a duty unless there is someone to whom it is due; there is no right unless there is someone from whom it's claimed; and there can be no wrong unless there is someone who's been wronged – in other words whose rights have been violated.

Other people say there are some duties without rights – for

example, duties towards the public at large, such as the duty not to commit a public nuisance. Who has a right there? You could of course say everyone has the right, for example, to use a public phone box without having to smell the public nuisance committed by a previous occupant the night before, but that's rather a different sort of right from saying that if a person puts 10 pence into the slot he has a right to make a phone call and British Telecom has a duty to put him through to the correct number. If you get the wrong number, you have the right to your money back (unless it's been excluded somehow); if you leave the phone box with your shoes and clothes so smelly that your best friends will only talk to you on the telephone, you can't sue the incontinent drunk who was responsible.

So there can be some duties without rights, provided you define duties fairly broadly. On the other hand, it's hard to see how there can be any rights without duties. If you've got a right, it must mean someone else has a duty to do (or not do) something.

## Hohfeld's correlatives

There once was a man called Wesley Newcombe Hohfeld (an American, as you'll have gathered). He's remembered (by those who remember him) for his analysis of rights. He wasn't satisfied that you could express even the most complicated legal ideas in terms of rights (and duties); some things weren't, strictly speaking, rights at all – they were privileges, powers, or immunities.

But how do you define a privilege, a power, an immunity? Hohfeld did it in a precise, almost mystical way. He started with rights and duties which he said were 'correlatives' of each other. By that he meant that they must always exist at the same time, though in different people: correlatives are the two ends of a single relationship, and when one person has one of the pair another person must have the other. A right is the correlative of a duty; a right is the presence of a duty in someone else.

What then is the correlative of a 'privilege'? Hohfeld said that it was 'no right'. A landowner has the privilege of ejecting trespassers; a trespasser has 'no right' to stay on the land.

But what is a privilege? This is where it gets awfully clever – though it's a bit hard to pick it up at first. A privilege is the opposite of a duty. Just as correlatives always exist together, opposites never exist together. They cancel each other out. Whereas correlatives are two things that always exist in different people, opposites are two things that never exist in the same person. To repeat, a privilege is the opposite of a duty. Thus a judge in court has the privilege of saying what he wants to because he's under no duty to observe the rules of defamation.

And just as privilege is the opposite of duty, right is obviously the opposite of 'no right'.

What we've got so far are four terms – rights, privileges, duties and 'no rights' – linked to one another either as correlatives or as opposites.

It gets even better when you move on to powers and immunities. Take the power to make a will. According to Hohfeld, it's not a right, because it doesn't involve a duty in someone else; and it's not a privilege, because if making a will was a privilege that would just mean it was something you could do without breaking the law. Making a will then, is a 'power'. And, said Hohfeld, the correlative of power is 'liability'. If you have the power to affect someone's legal rights, like a wealthy father who decides (so far as the law allows him) to cut off his child without a penny, the person affected is under a liability, such as the son who is liable to lose his inheritance.

Finally, 'immunities'. In the days when a peer could insist on being judged by his peers, he had no right in the strict sense, no liberty, and no power. What he did have was an immunity – an exemption from trial by jury. And the correlative of immunity is 'disability' or 'inability'. If a peer is immune to trial by jury, the jury is unable to try him. In other words, it has no power to try him.

Disability is therefore the opposite of power. Liability is the opposite of immunity. So the second set of four terms is connected in the same way as the first four terms.

If you've got this far without throwing the book at the cat you'll be wondering where all this is leading to. (If you have thrown the book at the cat, don't worry; cats don't have rights – or privileges, powers, or immunities. Yes, we know it's sometimes a criminal act to hurt a cat, but have you ever heard of a cat suing anybody? Children have rights, and people can sue on their behalf. But cats don't and can't.) To repeat – what's the point of Hohfeld?

One point is obviously that if you want to know what a power is, for example, you can define it in terms of the liability of someone else, or the disability which you, by definition, don't have. But this tends to be rather circular. Hohfeld intended his system to help people analyse problems more effectively by reducing complicated legal concepts to the lowest common denominator. It certainly does that, and if you can define problems accurately you're more likely to solve them correctly. But just as journalists often find that facts get in the way of a good story, students of jurisprudence tend to find that reality often intrudes on a good theory. Hohfeld's main fault seems to be that he takes everyday words and uses them in highly restricted ways. Some 'rights' can overlap between categories and even, as the law evolves, slide silently from one category to another. But if you have understood this part of the book, it should help you to think more clearly about what follows. And if all you remember about Hohfeld is that 'rights' can mean different things at different times and that giving someone a right means giving someone else an obligation, then you're not doing too badly.

## RIGHTS AND THE GOVERNMENT

So that's what a right is. Where does it come from?

Again, we're back to the problem that there's no written constitution to tell us the answer. Do rights come from the people? From the Crown? From the judges? From Parliament? From the government? From all of them?

Perhaps it doesn't really matter. It would be quite satisfying to propound a theory that all power resides in the breasts of the people, and that back in the mists of time and for the good of mankind we chose to hand it over to an all-powerful Monarch who is in turn given wise advice by the 'Lords Spiritual and Temporal, and Commons, in this present Parliament assembled', as the statutes put it. Alternatively and just as satisfyingly, you could say that at election time the people hand over power to their representatives in Parliament who, in turn, instruct the government through the legislative process on how to use this great power.

These theories are built on sand, of course, because power has never resided in the people. As Hartley and Griffith say in their book *Government and Law*, political power has instead resided in different groups of rulers who by reason of their military or economic strength have been able to wield it.

In practice, as Hartley and Griffith remind us, the government is not chosen by MPs. When we vote we are usually (though not always) voting for a party to govern the country, or even these days for a Prime Minister to lead that party – and not for an MP to represent us or to pass on his powers to a government. In any case, by the time Parliament assembles after the general election the new government has already started work.

So rather than spending time on any more theories, the remainder of this chapter will attempt to describe the system of government as it actually is. That should tell us where our rights really come from; how they can be taken away from us; and how we can even get new ones. Let's begin at the bottom.

The law on voting has just been changed. If proof were needed that even the most fundamental powers lie within the government (mainly) and Parliament (a bit), you only have to look at the new Representation of the People Act 1985.

Any government which can change the parliamentary franchise can change the composition of Parliament; any government which can create enough MPs to its own specifications can keep itself in power indefinitely. So perhaps it was with this in mind that the then Home Secretary pointed out when the Representation of the People Act received the Royal Assent in the summer of 1985 that in fact the government had 'had extensive consultations with the other parties, and as a result the bill ultimately achieved an unopposed third reading while still giving clear effect to the principles we were seeking to implement'.

## The Representation of the People Act 1985

The Act allows British citizens who used to live here but now live outside the United Kingdom to qualify as 'overseas voters' in the constituency where they were last registered – but only for a period of five years after they leave. The Home Office estimates that the new provisions will give up to half a million British citizens the right to vote at parliamentary and European Parliament (but not local government) elections. British citizens resident abroad will be able to register as overseas electors at British consulates from the summer of 1986. They will have the right to vote, by proxy, at any parliamentary or European Parliament election held after the 1987 register comes into force on 16 February 1987.

The Act introduces entirely new arrangements for people who are unable to vote in person at parliamentary, European Parliament and local government elections. The main change extends the right to apply for an absent vote at a particular election to all those (including holidaymakers) who cannot reasonably be expected to vote in person at the polling station. The Act also allows all absent voters to choose between proxy and, where the elector is within the United Kingdom during the period of the election, postal voting; all absent voters are allowed to vote by post or proxy at all local government elections in Great Britain, including parish and community council elections in England and Wales.

The right of blind and disabled electors and those whose occupation sends them away from home to go on a permanent list of absent voters is unchanged. The new arrangements are expected to come into effect in February 1987.

Candidates at parliamentary elections make a cash deposit which is refunded in full if the candidate polls more than a certain proportion of the total number of votes cast in the constituency.

The deposit stood at £150 from 1918 to 1985. The new Act increased the level to £500 but reduced the proportion of the total vote which the candidate must poll to keep his deposit from one-eighth to one-twentieth. The Home Office pointed out that £500 is less than one-quarter of the level at which the deposit would now stand if its value had kept pace with inflation.

The Act also allows the electoral registration officer to add the name of an elector he has left off by mistake. Often in the past such mistakes were only discovered when an election was imminent; it was then too late to amend the register even if the electoral registration officer was to blame. Another consequence of the Act is to allow the returning officer to begin counting ballot papers before all the ballot boxes have been received, which should lead to the results being declared up to an hour earlier than they used to be in some places.

## Taxation without representation

Talking of Representation brings us to Taxation – because (as the cliché has it) 'every schoolboy knows' there can be no taxation without representation. It's always rather gratifying to catch this supposedly omniscient and probably rather obnoxious schoolboy out: although Parliament passes a Finance Act every year, there are some major taxes which would still in fact be collected even if Parliament never met. We're not going to attempt in this book to give you even an outline of tax law or indeed to discuss whether the 'right' of citizenship is a correlative of the 'duty' to pay taxes. In reality, to quote Dicey again, 'the main point to be borne in mind is that all taxes are imposed by statute, and that no one can be forced to pay a single shilling by way of taxation which cannot be shown to the satisfaction of the judges to be due from him under Act of Parliament'. (Remember shillings? Nowadays even some undergraduates don't.) In terms of rights and duties, your duty is to pay your taxes to the government, and in return you have a right to the services – schools, roads, hospitals and so on – which the government provides.

The judges – who are taxpayers too of course – are fond of saying that there is no equity in a taxing statute. What that means is what Dicey was saying – if you're not covered by the precise wording of the Act, then you don't have to pay. Things are changing, and highly artificial schemes are no longer as acceptable to the courts as they were, but the main thing for ordinary folk to remember is the difference between tax avoidance and tax evasion. Tax avoidance is perfectly legal, and consists of arranging your affairs to take advantage of the system. Tax evasion involves making incorrect statements to the taxman which mislead him into undercharging. It's illegal.

Back then to our system of government. We're not going to bore you with a long explanation of parliamentary procedure, how a bill (normally) has to be approved by both Houses of Parliament before receiving the Royal Assent and thereby becoming law, how a private member's bill differs from a private bill, and so on. It's a fact of life that governments normally have majorities in the House of Commons and as a result can generally get their legislation on to the statute book.

But does this mean that whenever the government wants to create or destroy our rights it can do so? The answer is no.

## Power to the people?

In 1984 the Conservative government introduced into Parliament two major bills of special interest to lawyers. Each was reasonably uncontroversial; but each contained a niggling little clause which was bound to cause more trouble for the government than it was worth. Clause 22 of the Prosecution of Offences Bill would have given the Attorney General the invidious task of deciding whether to refer allegedly over-lenient sentences to the Court of Appeal. The court was not to be given any power to increase the sentence, but it would have been able to offer guidelines for the future. The proposal was a compromise, and ended up satisfying neither the Lord Chief Justice – who wanted the power to increase sentences on appeal – nor the Law Officers (the Attorney General and the Solicitor General), who wanted as little as possible to do with a power which would inevitably rebound on them however sparingly they used it.

That was a Home Office bill. The Administration of Justice Bill came from the Lord Chancellor's Department, which had inserted into it a clause that would effectively have made it less likely that a litigant who wanted to take action against a government department or public body could bring an action seeking judicial review of an official decision.

Both bills were introduced in the House of Lords and both clauses were eventually thrown out on a vote. The government could have reintroduced the clauses when the bills reached the House of Commons – and indeed with the government's huge majority they would no doubt have gone through. But then these Commons amendments would have had to go back to the Lords for approval, with the risk that peers might again have rejected the clauses. Rather than risk an unseemly row over two rather ill-thought out clauses, the government swallowed its pride, and accepted the will of the Upper House – while saying it would re-introduce clause 22 as part of the Criminal Justice Bill which is to be published at the end of 1986.

The point of these anecdotes is to show that even with a huge majority and a predominantly Conservative House of Lords, the government cannot always do exactly as it wishes.

An even more glaring example involves the Official Secrets Act. In 1979, for reasons we explain on page 111, the newly-elected Conservative government decided to repeal Section 2 of that Act and replace it with a Protection of Official Information Act. Shortly after the government's bill was first debated, it emerged that the much respected Surveyor of the Queen's Pictures, Sir Anthony Blunt, had been a Russian spy. That fact could not have been published if the bill had been law; as a result, the bill was rapidly dropped; and when challenged later, on its failure to reform the Official Secrets Act, the government maintained that its attempts had not met with the approval of Parliament. This of course was true but disingenuous; very little a government does meets with the support of every member of Parliament.

These examples of the role of Parliament in deciding what

rights we should have are conducted in the full glare of public scrutiny. Much less well known are the lobbyists.

## The lobbyists

One of the authors of this book produced a radio documentary about lobbyists, which was broadcast at the end of 1981 in the *Analysis* series on Radio 4. It had such an impact on one lobbying firm that when one of the firm's executives was telephoned by the BBC some weeks later he slammed the phone down as soon as he realised who he was speaking to. All the programme had said was that this firm published a brochure offering to arrange for promoting, opposing or amending legislation, briefing MPs at appropriate moments, suggesting useful parliamentary questions and encouraging unofficial 'interest' groups, and assisting with deputations and approaches to Ministers etc. The brochure also offered to help organise working lunches and dinners with specially selected MPs and peers. Another firm claimed to have saved the international motor car and motor-cycle industries based in the United Kingdom millions of pounds by persuading the government to exempt them from provisions in the Trade Descriptions Act, severely reduced demands on an American company for back payments of British excise duties, secured British Government planning permission for an oil platform building site, and so on.

None of this is illegal of course; it just ought to be better known. In 1982 a bill was introduced in the Commons by Bob Cryer, who was then an MP and who had taken part in the *Analysis* programme (though it would be wrong to assume he had been 'lobbied' by the BBC). His bill was designed 'to provide a public register of organisations who carry out the lobbying of Parliament for commercial gain' and for 'the disclosure of expenditure by such organisations'.

Like almost all bills introduced under the so-called Ten Minute Rule, it made no progress. The most these bills ever achieve is to stimulate public debate, but in June 1985 the Commons Select Committee on Members' Interests, which had been looking into the activities of Parliamentary lobbyists for more than a year, issued its report. It recommended that there should not be a register of professional lobbyists, but it said that journalists and research assistants at Westminster should have to declare any paid outside interests.

Occasionally lobbyists emerge blinking into the unaccustomed glare of publicity. One example in 1985 was that of a company of 'confidential political advisers and advocates to British business, trade and public bodies', as they described themselves, who were reported to have offered to pay £5,000 for a Commons select committee to fly to Sweden. There MPs were to see a new radioactive waste disposal scheme which uses large quantities of lead. The company, according to a report in *The Times*, acted for a group of international lead producers.

It's not just commercial organisations which go in for lobbying. Frank Field MP is still remembered for his campaign on behalf of the Child Poverty Action Group in the mid-seventies to replace family tax allowances with cash child benefits and have them paid direct to mothers. It achieved results, partly by persuading shadow ministers of the strength of its case so that when they moved from opposition into government they couldn't easily go back on what they'd said; partly by skilfully feeding the press with new aspects of the case; and above all by publishing in *New Society* in June 1976 leaked cabinet minutes which demonstrated how the new Prime Minister James Callaghan was intent on scuppering the whole scheme. That leak is still remembered by the staff at *New Society* who tried to flush the evidence down the lavatories (the ashes floated); it should also be remembered by the millions of parents who receive child benefit today.

From all this it seems clear that although the government will give way when confronted with a large enough group of MPs or peers, an individual lobbyist or pressure group can often be more effective than a lone back-bencher. But one should not underestimate the power of an MP as determined – some would say obsessive – as Tam Dalyell. Without his persistent questioning of ministers we would never have learned what we know today about how and why the *General Belgrano* was sunk during the

Falklands war. Indeed Clive Ponting, the former civil servant who was unsuccessfully prosecuted under the Official Secrets Act for sending Mr Dalyell documents about the sinking, says in his book *The Right to Know* that it had never occurred to him to leak the documents to anyone else, such as the newspapers. 'This was a matter for Parliament,' he writes. 'In the end ministers had to be responsible to Parliament or the whole British constitutional system would break down.'

But Tam Dalyell is an exception and not everyone who is against unnecessary government secrecy is as punctilious in observing constitutional proprieties. In a perfect world all back-benchers would be as effective as Tam Dalyell, and we'd be telling you at this stage in the book that just as every American citizen may some day become President, every British citizen over 21, who is not insane, nor a peer, nor bankrupt, nor convicted of treason, nor a Church of England or Church of Scotland or Roman Catholic clergyman, nor a judge, nor a civil servant, nor a serviceman, nor a police officer, nor on the board of a national-ised industry, nor a Governor of the BBC, and not disqualified for some other reason, may join a local political party, be adopted as its prospective parliamentary candidate, be elected to Parlia-ment, be elected to the leadership of that party and, if that party can command a majority in Parliament, be asked by the Queen to form a government. But life isn't like that, and you've probably got just as much chance of influencing events if you set out to be a journalist or a lobbyist. Otherwise why would MPs spend so much time talking to the two of us?

## SEPARATION OF POWERS

So far we've been talking, rather vaguely, about 'the government'. But that's only part of the story. To be sure we've dealt with all the people who can give us rights – and take them away – we must look in more detail at the three pillars of our constitution – the legislature, the executive, and the judiciary.

Before doing so we must get rid of what's called the doctrine of the separation of powers. And we mean 'get rid of'. It was Montesquieu who, after a visit to England in 1732, maintained that it was to the separation of powers that the English people owed their liberty: 'If the judicial power were joined with the legislative power,' he wrote, 'the power over life and liberty of citizens would be arbitrary, because the judge would be legislator. If it were joined to the executive power, the judge would have the strength of an oppressor. All would be lost if the same man . . . exercised these three powers, that of making laws, that of executing public decisions, and that of judging the crimes or the disputes of private persons.'

The problem with Montesquieu's superficially attractive theory is that it was based on a misunderstanding of the English constitution; it in turn has been misunderstood; and it bears no relation to our present constitutional system. It is not true to say that the legislature is the only body that legislates. It is not true to say that the executive is the only body that executes. It is not true to say that the judiciary is the only body that adjudicates. Nor should they be.

All this might seem rather disturbing to people who instinctively feel that these three bodies somehow 'ought' to keep to their primary powers; it may also disturb Americans whose constitution was based on the separation of the powers (although it has not stopped the Supreme Court from declaring laws passed by Congress invalid). But despite the overlapping of powers, democracy seems to have survived.

## The legislature

With that warning in mind, let's begin with the legislature. This in fact includes not only the House of Commons, not only the House of Lords, but also the Monarch. The Queen has to assent to all Acts of Parliament for them to become law. But of course she always does – it's a convention of the constitution, as we were saying earlier.

Dicey said the dominant characteristic of our political

31

institutions is the sovereignty of Parliament. By that he meant that Parliament has 'the right to make or unmake any law whatever; and, further, that no person or body is recognised by the law of England as having a right to override or set aside the legislation of Parliament'.

In other words, can Parliament do anything at all, anything perhaps except make a man into a woman and a woman into a man? No, says Sir Ivor Jennings, because 'if Parliament enacted that all men should be women, they would be women so far as the law is concerned. In speaking of the power of Parliament, we are dealing with legal principles, not with facts . . . . The supremacy of Parliament is a legal fiction, and legal fiction can assume anything.'

What Jennings is saying here is that even though Parliament has the legal power to do anything, there are some things which are politically impossible, which no Parliament would ever try to do. He quotes Laski's examples: 'no Parliament would dare to disfranchise Roman Catholics or to prohibit the existence of trade unions'. Laski might not have been so sanguine if he'd lived to see the ban in 1984 on trade unions at GCHQ, the Government's Communications Headquarters in Cheltenham, although, strictly speaking, that was a decision taken by ministers rather than by Parliament.

But just as there are things that no government would ask Parliament to do, there are things which some governments do ask Parliament to do, only to get no for an answer – such as the two 'niggling clauses' we mentioned on page 26. So the important thing to remember is that Parliament is not the government, and the government is not Parliament – however much governments, which do have a great deal of control over Parliament because they control its timetable, like to assume that Parliament is there to do exactly what they want. The 'government', in this sense, may include the Prime Minister, the cabinet, junior ministers who are not in the cabinet, and perhaps a few of the most senior civil servants. The fact that by convention ministers must be members of Parliament (either Commons or Lords) does not make the government identical with the legislature.

Every day of course the courts are asked to rule on the true meaning of laws made by Parliament. Sometimes they decide that a law does not mean what some people thought Parliament had intended it to mean. So is Parliament only sovereign to the extent that the courts will allow it to be?

The answer is no; although we'll have more to say about the powers of the courts to make law – to grant and take away rights – in a moment. The courts do not claim the power to repeal or overturn an Act of Parliament, while at the same time they acknowledge that Parliament has the power to reverse or overturn a decision of even the highest court in the land. So as between Parliament and the courts, Parliament wins in the end.

## The executive

The second of our three pillars of the constitution is the executive. Now this to all intents and purposes really is the government, which we've just defined as including the Prime Minister, all other ministers, and perhaps a few senior civil servants. We've spoken enough about the powers ministers have to propose legislation which on the whole is likely to get through Parliament. Ministers also have wide powers to make 'delegated legislation', as it's known: Parliament enacts the broad framework and allows the minister to make regulations from time to time which fill in the details. But these powers must not be exceeded; if they are, the courts will intervene.

More interesting – because less well-known – is the power of senior civil servants to shape policy without public scrutiny. Peter Kellner and Lord Crowther-Hunt, in their book *The Civil Servants* published in 1980, give examples of what they call 'questionable decision-making behind closed doors'. Frank Field's Child Benefit leak was one (see page 29); another was the decision to go ahead with Concorde in the 1960s; and then there was the breaking of oil sanctions against Rhodesia. In that case, they claim, a secret decision was taken in 1968, involving a member of the Labour government, civil servants, and oil companies, to

33

allow the oil companies to help arrange for oil to reach Rhodesia. 'The crux of the decision', they say, 'was a "swap" arrangement, whereby the French oil company Total sent oil into Rhodesia on behalf of the British companies Shell and BP. The details were negotiated between the oil companies and an Assistant Secretary at the Ministry of Power. The arrangement allowed Ministers to say that no British oil was reaching Rhodesia, although Parliament was never told what decisions had been reached.'

The lobbyists we spoke of earlier (page 28) make a particular point of lobbying civil servants. Another company offers 'the development of relevant contacts at all levels, up to senior officials', and yet another says their 'consultancy service deals primarily with putting over a particular case to the decision makers at Westminster and to their advisers in Whitehall'.

The BBC television series *Yes Minister*, written by Jonathan Lynn and Antony Jay, is described in the book of the film as 'Fiction/Comedy'. But in the light of what we've just been discussing, it would be wrong to write off completely their version (in 'The Bed of Nails') of ministries lobbying the government as a whole on behalf of client pressure groups. The book looks back on the civil service in the 1980s. The private secretary in *Yes Minister* has now become Sir Bernard Wooley GCB and recalls that 'every department acted for the powerful sectional interest with whom it had a permanent relationship. The Department of Employment lobbied for the TUC, whereas the Department of Industry lobbied for the employers. It was actually rather a nice balance: Energy lobbied for the oil companies, Defence lobbied for the armed forces, the Home Office for the police, and so on. . . . In other words, each Department of State was actually controlled by the people whom it was supposed to be controlling.'

Support for this rather cynical view of how things work comes from Robert McKenzie (he of the 'swingometer'), who wrote in 1974 that 'in no other country are the sectional interests . . . brought more intimately into consultation in the process of decision-making in government and political parties'. And Malcolm Davies, in his book *Politics of Pressure* (which expands on a BBC television series of the same name broadcast in 1985), notes

34

the close relationship between the National Farmers' Union and the Ministry of Agriculture. 'To its advantage and to the consequent disadvantage of its opponents', he writes, 'the National Farmers' Union is brought in at an early and formative stage in the discussion of new proposals. Conservation and environmental groups complain that the Wildlife and Countryside Bill of 1981 illustrates the advantages gained by a lobby group with incorporated status in that the main outlines of the Bill were decided amongst ministers, senior civil servants, the leaders of the National Farmers' Union and the Country Landowners' Association before the Bill was finally drafted.'

## The judiciary

The third pillar of the constitution is the judiciary. This is one area where the separation of the powers *is* said to apply, in that it is recognised that judges must be independent of the government. But how then do you explain the fact that the highest court in the land, the House of Lords, is constitutionally part of the legislature, and that even though Law Lords are specially appointed to hear cases, they can (and do) take part in the legislative proceedings of the Upper House? (By convention only the Law Lords take part in judicial proceedings, though on the fairly rare occasions when they sit in the Chamber itself – rather than in a committee room upstairs – other peers wander in, sit on the same red benches as the Law Lords, and listen, slightly bemused, to the proceedings.) What's more, how do you explain the role of the Lord Chancellor, who in one man combines all three powers: he presides over a branch of the legislature when he sits on the woolsack, he presides over a department of the executive when he sits as a government minister in the cabinet, and he presides over the judiciary when he sits as a Law Lord. Suffice it to say that our judges guard fiercely their independence from the government, although they see nothing wrong in chairing enquiries which sometimes appear to give support to the government's views (for example on whether telephone tapping is properly authorised) or discreetly asking the government to change the law (for example on making it more difficult to apply for judicial review).

## The judges as law-makers

Do judges make law? There are probably some judges who would still argue that they don't make new laws; they simply declare what the law has always been. In 1951 Lord Jowitt, who was then Lord Chancellor, said that if the common law (which simply means the accumulated decisions in previous cases) had produced a result which did not accord with the requirements of today, the answer would be to put it right by legislation. 'But,' said Lord Jowitt, 'do not expect every lawyer, in addition to all his other problems, to act as Lord Mansfield did and decide what the law ought to be. He is far better employed if he puts himself to the much simpler task of deciding what the law is.'

But another judge, Lord Radcliffe, said in 1968 that 'there never was a more sterile controversy than that upon the question whether a judge makes law. Of course he does. How can he help it? . . . The law has to be interpreted before it can be applied and interpretation is a creative activity.' But even Lord Radcliffe thought judges shouldn't let on. 'Men's respect for the law will be the greater,' he said, 'the more imperceptible its development.'

The greatest law-making judge of our times was of course Lord Denning. He summed up his views in *Discipline of Law*, the first in his annual series of 'holiday tasks' written in the long vacations. Lord Denning wrote that he was not against the doctrine of precedent. 'It is the foundation of our system of case law. . . . By standing by previous decisions, we have kept the common law on a good course. All that I am against is its too rigid application – a rigidity which insists that a bad precedent must necessarily be followed. I would treat it as you would a path through the woods. You must follow it certainly so as to reach your end. But you must not let the path become too overgrown. You must cut out the dead wood and trim off the side branches, else you will find yourself lost in thickets and brambles. My plea is simply to keep the path to justice clear of obstructions which would impede it.' The trouble with this, as Michael Zander says in his book *The Law-Making Process*, is that Lord Denning has never 'formulated principles to guide judges as to the kinds of cases in which they should intervene and when they should follow precedent and leave reform to the legislature'. Putting it another way, if you happen to agree with what Lord Denning thinks the law ought to be, that's fine. But if you happen to prefer the law as it was – especially if you've relied on the law as everyone had assumed it to have been – you may wish Lord Denning had followed precedent as much as other judges do.

So there we have the three great powers, the three pillars of our constitution. They must take the credit for giving us new rights and the blame for giving others new duties; they also carry the blame for taking our rights away and the credit for lifting the burden of duties from others.

## A RIGHT TO BREAK THE LAW?

Is there ever a right to break a 'bad' law? (And of course who's to say it's 'bad'?) Lord Denning has written about this too (in *The Mail on Sunday* at the end of 1984). He described deliberate breaking of the law by people who were doing it for their own ends as a disease clogging up the body politic. 'It needs a strong purgative to get rid of it,' Lord Denning said.

He gave the example of the shopkeepers who were then anticipating the repeal of the Shops Act by opening on Sundays. 'The stores rely on the law when it suits them, as in cases of shoplifting and fraud. They must observe the law when it does not suit them. They cannot pick and choose.' For Lord Denning there was only one answer to the question of whether this was a good law or not. 'Until it is repealed, it must be observed.' In Lord Denning's view the issue is clear and simple. 'Once we admit that there are occasions when it is proper, unilaterally, to decide that some laws may be broken, then we are on the road to certain doom.'

There are echoes here of something in Hobbes' *Leviathan*,

written when civil war was raging in England. Where there was no law or authority, wrote Hobbes, the life of man was 'solitary, poor, nasty, brutish and short'. And there are even louder echoes of a quotation Lord Denning himself used in 1977, and which became very much his own: 'to every subject in this land, no matter how powerful, I would use Thomas Fuller's words over 300 years ago: "Be you never so high, the law is above you" '.

So can there ever be a right to break a law you happen to disagree with? The first point to bear in mind is that you cannot always be sure what the law is until you get to court. Clive Ponting was accused of breaking the Official Secrets Act (as we saw on page 30); a jury found him not guilty. So there was no question of Clive Ponting breaking a 'bad' law; quite simply, Clive Ponting did not break the law.

That of course was a criminal case, and the outcome turned on its own particular facts. It comes within one of the meanings that Dicey gave to that much loved slogan 'the Rule of Law'; that 'a man may with us be punished for a breach of the law, but he can be punished for nothing else'.

Dicey's second elaboration of the Rule of Law was to exclude 'the idea of any exemption of officials or others from the duty of obedience to the law which governs other citizens or from the jurisdiction of the ordinary tribunals'.

Hartley and Griffith, writing ninety years later, make the same point when they say that those who rule must be subject to the law. 'For without this principle it would be impossible to challenge governmental action in the courts. As it is, no person or body of persons is exempt from action in the courts on the grounds of illegality and in such action every governmental body and the government itself must to avoid liability be able to point to some provision in the law if it wishes to claim a privileged position'.

What all this means is that governments and other public authorities aren't allowed to break laws either ('be you never so high . . .'). But it also reminds us that it is permissible for us to break a 'law' if that law isn't a law at all, because the government had no power to make it law. To prove that, you may have to bring a successful action for judicial review and show that a public authority acted beyond its powers (see page 57). For example when Labour took control of the Greater London Council in 1981 they cut London Transport fares by a quarter and ordered the London boroughs to raise a supplementary rate. One borough, Bromley, challenged the extra rate in the courts and won. As it happens, Bromley made the supplementary rate before taking legal action against the GLC. But if it had simply refused to obey the apparently lawful precept, and then been vindicated as indeed it was in the House of Lords, would it have been acting wrongly in refusing to obey a law which both it and the House of Lords considered 'bad'?

The practical problem for both Clive Ponting and the London Borough of Bromley was of course that there was no way they could be certain that the law was 'bad' until they had exhausted the legal process, and by then it might have been too late. But for anyone confident enough – or foolhardy enough – to believe that the law in question is not really the law at all, there can surely be no objection to a breach of that 'law'. For it's only by a legal challenge that a bad law can be exposed as such – and put right. And although the courts would deny any suggestion of retrospective law-making, they don't hesitate to declare that something done on a past occasion was illegal (a criminal offence) or unlawful (against the civil law) at the time in question – even if the individual involved reasonably believed otherwise and acted on that assumption. So if it is wrong to do something apparently legal which turns out later to have been illegal, surely it can't also be wrong to do something apparently illegal which turns out later to have been perfectly legal all the time?

## Natural justice

Can you go further and break a law because you think it is somehow immoral or improper, or against what you mean by the phrase 'natural justice' (though to lawyers – as you can see on page 60 – it might mean something rather more specific)? Take Nazi Germany as the classic example, where a law passed in June

1933 said anybody who committed an act 'which is deserving of penalty according to the fundamental conceptions of a penal law and sound popular feeling shall be punished'. Could anyone have been expected to respect a 'law' like that? But if it is acceptable to break such a law, what about our own wartime Defence Regulation 18B, which allowed the Home Secretary to detain anybody he had 'reasonable cause to believe to be of hostile origin or associations'? Wasn't that just as bad?

It certainly was to Lord Atkin in the famous case of *Liversidge v. Anderson* in 1942. He construed the regulation objectively, to mean, in effect, 'if there was reasonable cause to believe . . .' and said Liversidge was entitled to particulars of the grounds for the Home Secretary's belief. 'In this country, amid the clash of arms, the laws are not silent. They may be changed, but they speak the same language in war as in peace,' said Lord Atkin. 'I protest, even if I do it alone, against a strained construction put on words with the effect of giving an uncontrolled power of imprisonment to the minister.'

But as Lord Atkin said, he protested alone; all the other judges who heard the case decided Liversidge was not entitled to the particulars he'd requested. (Of course, if Liversidge had won, the government would immediately have changed the law to allow his detention to continue.)

## We plead guilty

Peacefully breaking the law is sometimes dignified with the title of 'civil disobedience'. Bertrand Russell and the Committee of One Hundred sat down in Trafalgar Square and were duly arrested. Their modern-day equivalents, the Peace Women of Greenham Common, break a Ministry of Defence by-law by trespassing on the air base; they too are arrested. Their aim is the same: to make governments listen – and act.

We too are guilty of civil disobedience. We – Rozenberg, Watkins, and our brave publishers at Dent – break the law on page 114 of this book by reproducing a government document without authority. Our aim is to reinforce the campaign, led by people immeasurably more distinguished than we are, to have Section 2 of the Official Secrets Act 1911 'pensioned off'.

We feel morally justified in doing this. We don't expect the Attorney General to prosecute us. But we admit we are breaking the law, and are prepared to face the consequences. We say it's a bad law. But you may ask what right we have to say that about the Official Secrets Act.

## Some practical problems

So the problem for those who assert a right to break a bad law is indeed the practical problem of who's to say it's bad. On the other hand, there are practical problems for those, like Lord Denning, who say there's never a right to break a bad law.

Take car parking. It's an offence to park a car anywhere on the road – even where there are no yellow lines or other regulations – if the parking causes 'unnecessary obstruction'. It's unclear whether you could get away in court with arguing that it's 'necessary' for you to have a car, 'necessary' to park it somewhere, and if you haven't got a garage of your own it's 'necessary' to park it in the street. But there must be many millions of motorists who've broken the road traffic legislation by illegal parking. Do they have a right to break a law which, as it stands, is silly, unenforcable, and unenforced?

Take a more serious example quoted by R.M. Jackson in his book *Enforcing the Law*. In December 1941, four thousand miners went on strike at Betteshanger Colliery in Kent. The strike was illegal under wartime regulations. The government wanted to prosecute all the men. It was decided to start with the only slightly more manageable figure of one thousand underground workers at the heart of the dispute. The union agreed, perhaps surprisingly, to tell its members to plead guilty and accept a decision on a few test cases. Only three union officials were sent to prison and the rest fined £1 each, with the alternative of 14 days imprisonment.

But then the problems began. The union officials were the only people who could call off the strike and they were in prison. An agreement, giving the men what they wanted, was duly

41

negotiated and signed in prison and the three officials were then released after serving only a few days of their sentences. The men went back to work, but only nine had paid their fines. The rest had refused. Were nearly a thousand men, working for the war effort, to be imprisoned in a county gaol which could only take a few at a time?

The management were so afraid of provoking another strike that they offered to pay the fines themselves. They were told not to do so and the court was simply instructed not to enforce the fines. (The nine who paid didn't get their money back, though.)

This then was clearly a bad law which depended for its effect on not being enforced. Using it brought the law into disrepute.

But the assertion that it can sometimes be right to break the law is linked much more closely to the miners' strike of 1984/85 than the one in 1941. In the book they edited for the Cobden Trust called *Policing the Miners' Strike*, Bob Fine and Robert Millar of the University of Warwick note that the Labour party's advice to the miners was to obey the law until Labour were in a position to change it. 'This option', says Fine and Millar, 'was painted as the exclusive way forward, but it offered little of immediate relevance to the miners and was rejected by their leaders in the NUM, who insisted on their right to break laws in defence of union rights.'

Fine and Millar seem to accept the NUM's reasoning: 'the state claims a monopoly on legitimate violence,' they write. 'This does not, however, entitle the state to use oppressive and arbitrary force. When it does – and this, we have argued, has been the case in the miners' strike – that monopoly of violence loses the legitimacy conferred on it under the rubric of the rule of law. These were the circumstances under which many miners asserted the right to defend their communities and their picket lines and to break the law.'

Now all that is fine as far as it goes, but it doesn't go very far. Where does this right to break the law come from? It is something, we are told, that many miners 'asserted'. Now if we, the authors of the book you're now reading, were to assert the right to reprint Fine and Millar's book and pocket the proceeds (perhaps because we agreed with their views, or perhaps because we disagreed), would we have that right? No? But perhaps the miners are different because there are more of them. So what if the official Soviet publishing house decided to do the same thing?

It's here that Hohfeld comes to the rescue. To assert a right means in this context to claim, unilaterally, a new right. But how can you have a unilateral right? There can only be a right if someone else has a duty. How can the miners impose a duty on others? If the others – in this case the State – were to acknowledge a duty, then the miners would be able to acquire a right. But if the State sits on its hands and does nothing, there's no way the miners can acquire a new right.

## No right to break the law

We share Lord Denning's view that there can never be a *right* to break the law. In practice you may get away with it. In some cases – such as the Official Secrets Act example, and parking in a side street without causing inconvenience to others – we think you should be able to get away with it. We could probably come up with plenty of moral arguments to support our position. But as we've said already, law and morality are not the same thing. If we had lived in Nazi Germany we would certainly have broken the law. If we had been striking miners we might have found it extremely difficult to observe the law. As it is, we don't find it very easy to keep to the 30 mile-per-hour speed limit in built-up areas; and there are one or two other little things we'd rather not mention at the moment. We wouldn't hesitate to use the law to establish our rights. But we still don't have the right to break the law.

# 2 *The courts*

There must be some people who have the good fortune to go through life without ever setting foot inside a court. At the opposite end of the scale are those adventurous types who, to take one example, delight in using the courts' ever-increasing powers to order judicial review of administrative decisions, a growth area in the law we'll be looking at later in this chapter. And between those two extremes are the sensible sorts who go to court when they have to – but not when they don't.

This is a book about rights. Rights are enforced in the civil courts and it's on these that we're going to concentrate. But we'll start with the criminal courts for two reasons: first, it's important to be absolutely sure of the difference between the two systems. And secondly because much of the next chapter – about civil liberties – is about the rights of people who may end up appearing before the criminal courts. So let's begin with a quick summary of the courts that deal with criminal cases.

## THE CRIMINAL COURTS

At the bottom of the hierarchy is of course the Magistrates' Court. The vast majority of magistrates are unpaid laymen (and of course lay women); there are also a few stipendiary magistrates who are legally qualified and paid to sit full time. Magistrates (also called Justices of the Peace or JPs) try minor criminal offences, and pass sentence on those they find guilty. More serious cases are dealt with by a judge and jury in the Crown Court (the Central Criminal Court – the Old Bailey – is a Crown Court). But even the most serious cases have to start in the Magistrates' Court, which traditionally had the job of deciding whether the prosecution had made out an arguable case against the defendant – in other words whether there's a case to answer. In practice, however, cases nowadays are usually committed for trial on the basis of written statements, and provided the defendant's lawyer doesn't object, the magistrates don't have to read and evaluate this sort of evidence. Crimes which are tried in the Magistrates' Court are called summary offences; those that have to be heard in the Crown Court are called indictable offences. A few are triable either way.

A defendant can appeal to the Crown Court against his conviction by the magistrates (unless of course he pleaded guilty). He can appeal against sentence whether he pleaded guilty or not guilty. If he thinks the magistrates got the law wrong he can appeal to the Queen's Bench Divisional Court (part of the High Court). Anyone who believes that the prosecution can never challenge an acquittal may be surprised to learn that the prosecution is also allowed to appeal to the Divisional Court on a point of law. For this purpose the magistrates are asked to 'state a case': in other words, to summarise the point to be decided by the Divisional Court. The judges can uphold the magistrates' decision, quash it, or order a rehearing.

Anyone convicted on indictment in the Crown Court may appeal to the Criminal Division of the Court of Appeal against the verdict, against the sentence, or on a point of law. Leave of the court is required unless the appeal is only on a point of law. An appeal to the House of Lords is only allowed on a point of law of general public importance, and again leave is required.

One of the most fascinating revelations of how Magistrates' Courts really work came from Dr John Baldwin, Director of the Institute of Judicial Administration at Birmingham University, in his recent book on *Pre-Trial Justice*. Dr Baldwin revealed an increasing tendency for the lawyers on each side of a case to meet 'well in advance of trial to determine the specific issues that are to be in dispute, the number of witnesses who will be required to address themselves to these issues and generally the course the trial will take. Though they are less ready to admit it,' writes Dr

Baldwin, 'the lawyers will also be keen to explore at the pre-trial review the possibilities of an out-of-court settlement through amicable compromise and accommodation'. In other words, where these pre-trial reviews are held the prosecution and defence lawyers will disclose their cases to one another with the result that in very many cases either the defendant will change his plea to guilty or the prosecutor will decide to drop at least some of the charges.

In May 1985, the government went one step further when it at last got round to using powers given to it by the Criminal Law Act of 1977. Rules made under the Act give people the right to see the prosecution evidence before their cases are dealt with by the magistrates. The rules don't apply to cases which can only be tried in the Magistrates' Court. In the more serious cases tried by a jury the defence already gets details of the prosecution case. So what the new rules do is to extend this right to cases triable either way. It is up to the defendant to ask for the information; at the moment the prosecution has the choice of disclosing either a summary of the case or copies of statements made by witnesses. The Home Office said when the changes were announced that once some defendants realised the strength of the case against them, they'd decide to plead guilty. Before the new rules were introduced, defendants whose cases were triable either in the Magistrates' Court or in the Crown Court asked for jury trial just to see the statements; they would then either get permission to have the case heard by the magistrates after all, or go on to plead guilty in the Crown Court, which was seen as a waste of time and resources. There are signs that the new procedure is already saving time and money.

By now you'll have gathered how the criminal courts differ from the civil courts. To sum up, in criminal cases a defendant is prosecuted by the prosecutor; in the civil courts a defendant is sued by the plaintiff. In a criminal matter the defendant will only be found guilty if the case is proved beyond all reasonable doubt; in a civil action the standard of proof is lower – the defendant will have judgment entered against him (in other words, he'll lose the case) if the plaintiff proves his case on the balance of probabilities.

# THE CIVIL COURTS

## *The County Courts*

Just as most criminal cases are dealt with by the Magistrates' Courts, most civil cases are dealt with by the County Courts. You might reasonably think there'd be one in each county, or one in the county town perhaps, or that they'd be run and paid for by the county council, or at the very least that they'd have something to do with the counties of England and Wales. You'd be wrong. Nowadays it's just a name.

When the County Courts were set up in 1846 they were seen as a simple way of dealing with small claims. At present, the maximum sum of damages you can claim is £5,000 – which is not so small – and in some circumstances the amount disputed can be a good deal higher. So now there is a special procedure for dealing with really small claims – which at present means not worth more than £500. (You might hear people referring to this as suing in 'the small claims courts'. Strictly speaking this is wrong – it's the same County Court whether it's dealing with a small claim or a large claim. There have been 'small claims courts' set up which are not courts at all – merely organised systems of arbitration which do not in themselves have the powers of a court.)

But what are 'small claims'? Here's a list of the main small claims in the County Court:

(1) Claims for payment of debts, whether for goods sold, work done, or money lent.

(2) Claims arising out of the sale of goods, including the repair of damaged goods, failure to supply goods ordered or supplying the wrong article or a defective one.

(3) Claims against people providing consumer services, such as garages, dry cleaners, repairers of electrical and other goods in respect of faulty workmanship or failure to do the work that was agreed.

(4) Claims for possession of property, arrears of rent, return of

47

deposits or other disputes between landlords and tenant. (With the possible exception of claims for arrears of rent, the return of deposits or for possession of furnished premises, it is advisable to obtain legal advice before starting proceedings on your own.)

(5) Claims for damages caused by negligence, such as a claim arising out of a road accident. Usually these are covered by insurance, but where the amount is less than the excess on a policy or the insured has only third party cover or does not want to risk his 'No claims bonus', he may wish to sue the other driver. (If the damage is substantial or personal injuries are involved you should consult a solicitor.)

(6) Claims for damages for wilful damage to property or for assault. (In cases of injury requiring medical attention you should consult a solicitor.)

(7) Claims for wages or salary owing or payable in lieu of notice.

This list comes from an excellent booklet called, inevitably, *Small Claims in the County Court*. It was written by Michael Birks, former Registrar of the West London County Court, and now a judge; you can get a free copy from your local County Court or from the Lord Chancellor's Department, Neville House, Page Street, London SW1P 4LS.

The booklet begins with a word of warning – the modern equivalent of the wartime slogan 'Is your journey really necessary?' The warning points out that there is little satisfaction to be gained from winning an action if your opponent has no money to pay the judgment debt. 'The principal purpose of this guide is to tell you how to sue in the County Court', it says; 'whether it is worth your while to do so is another matter'.

This warning has a still wider application. People often come up to us and ask whether they have the right to do this or the right to do that. You may have bought this book with the same question in mind. As lawyers we can tell you whether we think you have rights. But only you can decide whether you want to enforce them. One of us knows a lady who's managed at various times to get involved in petty legal disputes with both her neighbours. Should we have advised her to sue? Or shouldn't she rather think of the bitterness and acrimony that could result from a dispute with the person living next door? Every legal journalist receives a sad file of documents from time to time. It includes copies of letters to the Queen, the Prime Minister, the Lord Chancellor; there's usually a well-preserved and much-underlined press cutting from a local newspaper; and despite voluminous correspondence going back many years the original problem seems no nearer a solution. The people who send these problems to journalists (and sometimes try to persuade solicitors to take them up) say that all they're looking for is 'justice'. They feel that this is their right and that if they keep on fighting for it they will eventually achieve it. How one longs to tell them to give up before their fight for justice sends them gently round the bend. How one longs to tell them that our legal system is imperfect, that the just do not always get justice, that life is full of compromises and a shrewd man is one who knows when to cut his losses.

But we're not talking about you, are we; you'd just like to know a bit more about how to sue in the County Court. And there's also the rather delicate question of whether you need a solicitor.

Let's assume your claim is for less than £500. Normally if you win your case you can expect the other side to be ordered to pay your legal costs. But if your claim is under £500, then as a rule you will have to pay your own expenses even if you win. It also works the other way: if you lose your case you won't have to pay your opponent's legal costs if the claim is below £500. There is an exception, though: when you begin proceedings, you have to pay the court a fee – at present it's 10p for every £1 you claim, with a minimum fee of £6; and a maximum fee of £40 for all claims over £500. Assuming you're claiming more than £60, it works out at 10 per cent; so, for example, the court fee on a claim of £100 is £10 – which is not to be sneezed at. The only consolation is that although you won't get your costs reimbursed in a small claim, if it was you who began the proceedings and you win your case the loser may be ordered to pay you the money you spent on court fees.

So should you have a solicitor? Take the example of a claim for £100 again. If your solicitor charges you £100 for his work in getting the money back then you're not a penny better off even if you win. If it makes you feel better to think your opponent 'hasn't got away with it', ask yourself whether you could have reached a deal with him or her to split the difference. Wouldn't it be better for you to have £50 and let your opponent keep £50 rather than give the lawyer £100?

It's clear then that the system is designed to discourage you from using a solicitor in small claims. How easy is it for you to act by yourself? The official advice in *Small Claims in the County Court* is that 'the formalities are kept to the minimum and you should have no difficulty in handling your own case'.

While that's true, you should bear in mind that it's possible to take advice from a solicitor in the early stages of a dispute without committing yourself to instructing a solicitor later on. Half an hour with a solicitor who deals with litigation might be all that's needed to steer you in the right direction, and if you're eligible for legal aid (or more accurately legal advice) under what's called the 'Green Form' scheme it could cost you little or nothing. (Legal Aid is dealt with on page 69.) If you're not eligible for legal aid you may find a solicitor who has agreed to charge only £5 for half an hour's advice. Solicitors who've said they're prepared to do this are named in the Solicitors Regional Directory available from libraries and Citizens' Advice Bureaux. Or try your local law centre.

In general, whether you use a solicitor is up to you (and perhaps your bank manager). There are many things which you as a non-lawyer will manage eventually but which a solicitor can do as a matter of pure routine. No book – certainly not this one – can tell you all the law; it may have changed, or there might be obscure provisions you won't have come across. Perhaps your solicitor will. If you lose your case through your own ignorance you'll have nobody to sue. Solicitors carry insurance. On the other hand there are many things an intelligent layman can do just as well as, if not better than, a harassed solicitor. In the end, it all comes down to money. Even if you can do the job, are you prepared to pay for the convenience of having somebody else do it for you? Most people can cook, but they still enjoy eating in restaurants from time to time. What they don't like are meals that are over-priced and underdone.

## How to sue in the County Court

Let's assume that you're determined to start proceedings in the County Court for a claim worth not more than £500. You've started by writing a firm letter to the person you're planning to sue, inviting him or her to pay up and threatening to sue if they don't. (It's a good idea incidentally to name the County Court in which you'll be issuing proceedings – it gives the impression you know what you're doing. You have to sue in the court covering the area where the defendant lives or works; alternatively you can use the court for the district where the events giving rise to the claim happened. County Courts are usually listed in the phone book under C for courts.)

If there's no response to your letters it's at this stage that you visit the court, collect your free copy of the booklet on *Small Claims*, and study it carefully. The booklet explains how you have to write out particulars of your claim which explain why you are taking action and how much you are claiming. Nowadays you can also claim interest. You used to have to fill in a form called, not unreasonably, a 'request'. (Before that it was called a 'praecipe' which was much more unreasonable.) In return the court staff used to prepare a summons to serve on the defendant. Now, in a move towards do-it-yourself justice, you can fill in the summons form yourself and hand it in to be rubber-stamped by the court. It's then served. But the old procedure is still available if you prefer to use the request form. You also have to pay the court fee and in return you get a plaint note which bears the all-important number of your action.

If you're claiming money, the court will issue a default summons. This gives the defendant a fortnight either to admit your claim and offer to pay, or to file a defence to the action. If he doesn't do anything, you can ask the court to enter judgment by default. If the defendant makes an offer which you don't accept, tell the court and an appointment will be fixed for the court registrar to decide how the debt is to be paid. If the defendant files a defence, the court will then arrange a pre-trial review, or the trial itself. (The word 'trial' is used for civil cases as well as criminal cases.) You can have judgment entered in default even if you're not claiming a fixed sum of money. The judgment will then be for 'damages to be assessed' and the court will decide the amount later.

If you're not claiming money, the court will issue a fixed date summons, ordering the defendant to attend court on a specified date, usually about six weeks away, for a pre-trial review.

The pre-trial review is informal and friendly. It's normally held in the registrar's private room. If the defendant hasn't turned up you may be able to prove your case there and then or the registrar may simply enter judgment for you. If the defendant has come, the registrar may ask you or the defendant for more information. He may even be able to help you reach an agreement with the defendant to settle the case. Don't forget to bring all your papers.

Failing that, the registrar will make arrangements for the trial or arbitration. As we've said, arbitration is normal for claims up to £500, though it can be ordered for larger claims and it's possible for claims of not more than £500 to be tried in court if there are difficult questions of fact or law, or if arbitration would be unreasonable for some other reason.

A trial is much more formal than an arbitration. A trial is held in a public courtroom while an arbitration is private. The rules of evidence are applied more strictly at a trial.

As we said earlier, you can't claim solicitors' fees if you win a small claim. But you can recover court fees, witnesses' expenses (you were probably a witness in your own case), and some other expenses you've had to lay out.

## What to do when you've won your case

Winning your case can be easy, especially if the defendant doesn't turn up. Getting your money can be much more difficult, especially if the defendant hasn't got any. People think that once the court has made an order, their money will come jingling through the letter box. But that's not the way it works. The court won't pay. It will do nothing unless you ask it to. And whatever it does costs money – sometimes quite a lot.

Michael Birks' slim volume *Small Claims in the County Court* was such a Number One Bestseller that he's written a sequel called, inevitably, *Enforcing Money Judgments in the County Court*. This begins with an 'I told you so' reminder of his earlier advice not to sue people who can't pay, and a further warning about the pointlessness of enforcing judgments against people with no money. (Even if they've got the cash it's sometimes difficult to get hold of it, as four sequestrators discovered when they tried to get hold of money belonging to the National Union of Mineworkers in 1984.)

Armed with this guide (also obtainable free from County Courts and the Lord Chancellor's Department) you can learn how to send in the bailiff to seize the debtor's goods (full of pitfalls); how to get an Attachment of Earnings Order (if you know where the debtor works); how to obtain the wonderfully named garnishee order to freeze the debtor's bank account (if he's not already overdrawn); how to obtain a charging order on land (very complicated); and how to call in a receiver (very difficult without a solicitor).

## How to be sued in the County Court

Some people who receive summonses (and income tax demands, dentists' appointments, renewal notices from the library and the like) ignore them in the hope they'll go away. They won't. Do something, even if it's only to call in a solicitor.

Of course, just as it's possible to sue in the County Court without a solicitor there's nothing to stop you from handling by yourself any summons you may receive. But the advice we gave on page 50 to people who want to sue applies equally to those being sued – even down to getting a copy of the free booklet *Small*

*Claims in the County Court.* Whatever you do, though, read the summons carefully and do what it says. Either pay the money into court (not to the person who's suing you), or ask for time to pay, or file a defence on the form provided (but only if you really do have a defence) and don't forget to turn up at the pre-trial review if there is one. But if you have failed to do what's necessary, don't despair. It's even possible to have a judgment set aside if you've got a good enough reason. But above all don't put it off; nobody likes being ignored and courts are no exception. So if you do nothing else, go along to the court office (the address is on the summons) and ask the staff for help. If you're nice to them they'll be nice to you; they'll explain things and help you fill in the forms. But of course what they can't do is give you legal advice, in other words tell you if you've got a good case and advise you on tactics. That would give you an unfair advantage over your opponent.

## Arbitration

As we've said, small claims in the County Court are normally dealt with by arbitration. But arbitration is not confined to the County Court. The Chartered Institute of Arbitrators (75 Cannon Street, London EC4N 5BH, telephone 01–236 8761) runs a small claims arbitration service for companies which want it (and are prepared to pay for it). The Association of British Travel Agents uses the scheme, and you can read more about this in our section on holidays (page 180). But it's also used by companies in the motor industry, communications and insurance (the 'Personal Injury Arbitration Service').

This is how it works. You, the consumer, have ordered goods or services under a contract with a company that offers arbitration to deal with disputes. Something has gone wrong and you've not been able to sort it out with the company. It's then up to you whether you take legal proceedings in the court or go to arbitration. If you decide on arbitration you have to agree to be bound by the arbitrator's decision.

Under the small claims arbitration scheme there's no oral hearing. Instead you (and the company) send in a claim form.

Both sides send in their documents (each gets to see the other's). Each side pays a fee (£17.25 for claims up to £2,500 – which for large claims is much less than you'd pay in the County Court). The arbitrator reads the documents, makes up his mind, and sends you his decision by post. The loser then has three weeks to pay up. The loser may also have to pay the winner's arbitration fee, as well as his own. What this means is that if you go to arbitration, and lose, the most it's going to cost you is double the registration fee – £34.50 on claims up to £2,500. As well as being pretty cheap, it's informal and there's no need to take time off to attend court. But if the facts may be in dispute, or the case involves difficult legal issues or a sum of money you could ill afford to lose, it would be a good idea to take legal advice on whether you'd be better off going to court rather than to arbitration.

Insurance claims can only be referred to the Personal Insurance Arbitration Service if the company agrees. You too have to agree to be bound by the decision. As an alternative, try the Insurance Ombudsman Bureau (31 Southampton Row, London WC1B 5HJ, telephone 01–242 8613). He too will arbitrate, but if you're unhappy with his decision you can still take your case to court.

## The High Court

Big, important and difficult civil cases are dealt with by the High Court. (You can use the High Court for small claims if you really want to, but it will be very expensive even if you win, so it's not a good idea.)

The High Court is split into three divisions. The one most likely to get reported on radio and in the newspapers is the Queen's Bench Division, which deals with claims based on contract, tort (a tort is a civil wrong where no contract is involved, such as negligence) and claims for recovery of land. The Queen's Bench Division also includes the Commercial Court and the Admiralty Court.

The Family Division of the High Court, being quite new, has a name that means something to non-lawyers. It deals with

defended divorces, which are fairly rare (as opposed to undefended divorces where there are disputes over money or children
which are much more common and are dealt with in the County
Court); the Family Division also deals with some disputes over
children. The Family Division is not a Family Court. The idea of
having one court to deal with all aspects of family law is discussed
on page 146.

The remaining division of the High Court is the Chancery
Division. It deals with trusts, wills, settlements and other cases
stemming from the rules of equity rather than the common law. It
would be unfair (and wrong) to think nothing has changed since
Charles Dickens wrote about the Court of Chancery in *Bleak
House*. But a report in 1960 said drawing up Chancery orders
involved 'just as we have seen they did in 1826 and 1874,
unnecessary expense'. The report of the Committee on Chancery
Chambers went on to say it seemed likely 'that the telephone is
less used in the High Court than in any other office in the
Kingdom'. Writing about this in 1967, R.M. Jackson says in a
footnote to *The Machinery of Justice in England*: 'In earlier
editions I said that officials concealed their telephone numbers. I
did not then know that on the Chancery side there was but a single
telephone and that was not ordinarily used: it was installed in case
the Lord Chancellor should want to phone.' Incidentally,
although the Lord Chancellor, as his title would suggest, is
nominally head of the Chancery Division, the senior judge in
practice is the Vice-Chancellor. Sir Nicolas Browne-Wilkinson
was appointed Vice-Chancellor in 1985, but retains his right to sit
as a Lord Justice of Appeal in the Court of Appeal.

## The Divisional Courts

Each of the three divisions of the High Court includes a rather
confusingly named Divisional Court to deal with appeals. You
probably won't hear much about the Family Divisional Court
which deals with appeals from Magistrates' Courts and Juvenile
Courts in domestic and matrimonial matters; still less will you
come across the Chancery Divisional Court which takes bank-

ruptcy appeals from the county courts. But the Queen's Bench Divisional Court is important. We've already said it hears criminal appeals from the Magistrates' Courts which raise a point of law. It's also the court that normally deals with applications for the writ of *habeas corpus ad subjiciendum*, ordering the release of anyone unlawfully detained. But in terms of the development of English law perhaps the most important role of the Queen's Bench Divisional Court nowadays is to hear applications for judicial review.

## Judicial review – the law

This is a complicated area of the law and is changing rapidly. Mr Justice Woolf said recently that since the rules were changed in 1977 the growth of judicial review has been 'explosive'. In practice the judges have a great deal of discretion in balancing the needs of the administration against the rights of the citizen. So it's impossible in a book like this to predict how a particular problem will be decided by the courts; the most we can do is to explain what sort of cases are dealt with and to mention a few of the key principles applied by the courts.

Mr Justice Woolf's remarks about the growth of judicial review will be endorsed by any journalist whose beat includes the Law Courts in London. The judge was writing an introduction to a new book called *Judicial Review* by Kenneth Bagnall QC. (It's published by a firm called Profex of Trafalgar House, Grenville Place, London NW7 3SA and can be found in specialist legal bookshops. Another new book on *Applications for Judicial Review* is the one by Grahame Aldous and John Alder.) Mr Justice Woolf says the system of applying for judicial review 'provides a means by which a litigant can with the greatest of ease and at nominal cost ascertain whether a High Court judge considers he has a prima facie case'. He suggests that, with the help of Kenneth Bagnall's book, the inexperienced litigant should have no difficulty in filling in the forms to establish whether or not his case is arguable. But a word of warning is necessary here. All the judge is saying is that it's possible for a non-lawyer to attempt the first hurdle – getting leave; he's not saying (and nor would we) that you should try to handle the whole application for judicial review without legal advice (or without the advice of a solicitor who has quickly mugged up on one of these books). And although the 'nominal cost' of applying for leave is £10, another £45 is required when you begin proceedings in earnest.

What then is judicial review? Put simply, it's a way of overturning the decisions of a public body which has used powers that it hasn't got.

One of the most important recent cases on judicial review is known to lawyers as *In re the Council of Civil Service Unions and others*, though of course everyone else calls it the GCHQ case. You'll remember that in November 1984 trade unions at the Government Communications Headquarters in Cheltenham lost their appeal to the House of Lords against the government's decision to withdraw trade union rights from staff there. The five law lords who heard the case decided unanimously that the government's action was justified on grounds of national security. (The unions were not ordered to pay the government's costs though, and in May 1985 they started proceedings at the European Commission of Human Rights in Strasbourg.) But even though judicial review was refused, the lords took the opportunity – as you might expect – to outline the current state of the law. Unfortunately, the more important a case is, the more of the law lords there are who feel impelled to offer their own views on it. In this case all five judges delivered speeches, and this can sometimes make it harder to 'extract the ratio', as lawyers say when they mean 'understand what the case decided'. But for our detailed explanation of judicial review we'll be relying mainly on Lord Diplock, garnished with the occasional gloss from Lord Roskill.

Lord Diplock began by saying that in every case of judicial review there's a decision made (or refused) by a 'decision-maker'. To qualify for judicial review the decision must affect someone else, either by altering his rights (or duties); or by depriving him of some benefit which he's had in the past and can legitimately expect to have in the future. The decision-maker must have been given his powers under public law (unlike an arbitrator). Lord

Diplock then said there were three grounds on which administrative action of this sort is subject to control by judicial review. He gave them new names: 'illegality', 'irrationality' and 'procedural impropriety'. We'll look at each of them in turn.

By saying that a decision could be overturned on grounds of 'illegality' Lord Diplock meant that the decision-maker must understand correctly the law that regulates his power to make decisions and give effect to it. If the decision-maker has got the law wrong and purports to exercise a power he doesn't have, then it will be illegal and the judges will use judicial review to overturn the decision. This of course is a new name for our old friend *ultra vires* (a phrase not mentioned in the GCHQ judgment). That was simply the principle that a public authority must not exceed its powers (in other words, act *ultra vires*). Before GCHQ, the *ultra vires* principle was said to prevent public authorities from doing anything the law forbids, or taking any action for which they have no statutory authority. But Lord Diplock's 'illegality' seems to amount to pretty much the same thing.

By 'irrationality' Lord Diplock meant the sort of decision that is 'so outrageous in its defiance of logic or of accepted moral standards that no sensible person who had applied his mind to the question to be decided could have arrived at it'. If you spend any time listening to cases of judicial review you'll hear this referred to as 'Wednesbury-unreasonable'. You may wonder why a perfectly harmless West Midlands town between Birmingham and Wolverhampton should be stigmatised as the epitome of unreasonableness, perhaps for one lapse long ago. But if you look up the case of *Associated Provincial Picture Houses Ltd v. Wednesbury Corporation* (reported in 1948) you'll find that Wednesbury Corporation behaved perfectly reasonably and in fact judicial review was refused. The details of the case seem to come from a different world. What happened was that the local cinema in Wednesbury wanted to open on Sundays. To do so it had to get a licence from the Council, which could be granted 'subject to such conditions as the authority think fit to impose'. Wednesbury Council imposed the condition that no children under fifteen would be allowed in on a Sunday. The cinema said this was an unreasonable condition. The Court of Appeal said it was not. 'Nobody', said the Master of the Rolls, Lord Greene, 'could say that the well-being and the physical and moral health of children is not a matter which a local authority, in exercising their powers, can properly have in mind, when those questions are germane to what they have to consider'.

What the *Wednesbury* case actually decided was that a decision-maker who has to exercise a discretion must have regard to matters to which he is referred by the statute giving him the discretion; he must ignore irrelevant considerations; he must not operate on the basis of bad faith or dishonesty; he must direct himself properly in law, and he must act as any reasonable person would act and not be so absurd in his actions that no reasonable person would act in that way. To do otherwise is 'Wednesbury-unreasonable'; or, as Lord Diplock and no doubt the good people of Wednesbury would prefer, 'irrational'.

Lord Diplock's third ground for granting judicial review is 'procedural impropriety'. This is his new name for what used to be called a breach of 'natural justice'. Now natural justice is a wonderful phrase, much used by people who don't know what it means. After all, what is 'natural' about justice? Used by lawyers, the phrase had two specific meanings. Being lawyers, they expressed them in Latin. They are *audi alteram partem* ('hear the other side') and *nemo judex in causa sua* ('nobody can be a judge in his own cause'). The *audi alteram partem* rule granted the right to a fair hearing; it meant that nobody could be penalised by a decision-maker unless he'd been given notice of the case he had to meet and an opportunity to be heard. The *nemo judex in causa sua* rule was no more than a rule against bias – that an adjudicator must not have a direct interest in the outcome of the proceedings; nor was he to be reasonably suspected of bias. When Louis Blom-Cooper QC appeared for the civil service unions in the GCHQ case he avoided the phrase 'natural justice'; instead he spoke simply of the procedural obligation to act fairly. But even that phrase is rejected by Lord Diplock. Procedural impropriety, in his definition, goes further than a breach of natural justice and includes failure by an administrative tribunal to observe rules of procedure laid down by Parliament when it set the tribunal up.

But whether you speak of procedural impropriety (as Lord Diplock) or the duty to act fairly (as Lord Roskill), it's at this point that 'reasonable expectations' appear on the scene. In Lord Roskill's words, a person may be entitled to judicial review 'if he can show that he had "a reasonable expectation" of some occurrence or action preceding the decision complained of and that that "reasonable expectation" was not in the event fulfilled'. The phrase 'legitimate expectation' apparently means the same thing as 'reasonable expectation'.

Judicial review is subject to one very important limitation. Aldous and Alder, writing in 1985, say that the Divisional Court 'cannot determine whether decisions are right or wrong on their merits'. They add that judicial review 'is not an avenue for appeal against decisions'. Indeed Lord Fraser of Tullybelton said in the GCHQ case that the issue was not whether the minister's instruction was 'proper or fair or justifiable on its merits. These matters are not for the courts to determine. The sole issue is whether the decision . . . was reached by a process that was fair to the staff at GCHQ.' And Lord Fraser quoted Lord Brightman, who said in another case, 'judicial review is concerned not with the decision, but with the decision-making process'.

Recent though these statements of the law are, there are signs they may already be getting a little out of date. The courts appear to be enlarging on their powers to the extent that some judges seem to be prepared to look at the merits of a case, as the United States courts do in cases of judicial review. It seems too soon to rely on persuading a judge to look at the merits of a decision rather than the way in which it was taken, but some lawyers say that this, in effect, is what is now happening more and more.

From time to time law students have been driven to write letters to the judges asking them – only half in jest – to stop creating any more new laws until after the exams are over. Judicial review is just one of those areas. The principles of legitimate or reasonable expectation we've just mentioned are very new, although the phrase 'legitimate expectation' was first used by Lord Denning (who else?) as long ago as 1969. And Lord

Diplock said in the GCHQ case that further development of judicial review on a case-by-case basis may in the course of time add further grounds. He was thinking particularly of the possible adoption in the future of the principle of 'proportionality' which is recognised in the administrative law of several continental countries. Who said judges don't make new law?

## Judicial review – how to get it

Applications for the various sorts of judicial review – mandamus, prohibition and certiorari – used to be rather complicated. Now you just ask for leave to apply for judicial review under Order 53 of the Rules of the Supreme Court. There's a form (86A) to be completed and you'll have to swear an affidavit in support. If you get leave to apply for judicial review, you then fill in and serve a notice of motion (Form 86). The forms and some basic notes for guidance can be obtained from the Crown Office at the Royal Courts of Justice, Strand, London WC2A 2LL (01–936 6205). But despite the remarks of Mr Justice Woolf quoted earlier, we think you'd have to be a pretty exceptional litigant to conduct a case involving judicial review without professional help, or at least one of the books we mentioned earlier.

# THE APPEAL COURTS

## The Court of Appeal

The civil division of the Court of Appeal in London hears appeals from the High Court, the County Courts, and a few other tribunals. Its head is the Master of the Rolls, Sir John Donaldson. Its previous decisions are binding on the courts below – and, generally speaking, on itself. Hearings, though important, don't mean much to non-lawyers; it's all legal argument and the witnesses don't give evidence again.

The criminal division of the Court of Appeal hears appeals

from defendants convicted in the Crown Court. It can overturn a conviction or reduce the sentence. The head of the Criminal Division is the Lord Chief Justice, Lord Lane. Although the prosecution can't appeal against an acquittal, there is a little-known procedure whereby the Attorney-General can refer a case to the Court of Appeal for an authoritative ruling on the law. But whatever the Court of Appeal decides, the defendant stays acquitted.

## The House of Lords

Most people know that the House of Lords is the highest court in the land. This is true, but only part of the truth. To take a case to the Lords you need the permission of either the Court of Appeal or the Lords themselves, and in criminal cases the Court of Appeal must also certify that the case involves a point of law of general public importance. What's more, the House of Lords does not hear criminal appeals from Scotland. So in practice the final court in the great majority of cases tends to be the Court of Appeal. That, incidentally, was one reason why Lord Denning stepped down from the House of Lords to become Master of the Rolls: it gave him more influence.

When we talk of the House of Lords as a court, what we really mean is the Appellate Committee. As we said on page 35, in constitutional theory the House of Lords which hears cases is the same House of Lords as the one that debates legislation. But in practice the Law Lords who make up the Appellate Committee are judges who are specially appointed to the job. While Law Lords take part in general debates, peers who are not Law Lords never dare take part in judicial proceedings.

If you're sufficiently interested in legal affairs to be reading this book, you should drop in on the Appellate Committee next time you're in Westminster. It will come as a bit of a shock. The court generally sits in a room at the end of the almost endless committee corridor. It's not a big room and the five Law Lords sit at little tables looking up at counsel rather than down from a great height as in other courts. What's more, the judges wear ordinary grey suits rather than robes; and they don't even wear wigs. The barristers who appear before them are dressed normally (if you can call a wig and gown normal) and, on the rare occasions when the Law Lords sit in the Chamber, Queen's Council have to wear full-bottomed wigs. (These are the wigs that cover your ears and flap round your shoulders – the sort that cartoonists wrongly believe judges wear all the time.)

The Law Lords produce their judgments (called 'speeches') on a word processor and hand them out instead of reading them. This makes them much easier to report. The Court of Appeal and even the High Court have started making copies of their judgments available to the press but the system there is sometimes erratic and there aren't always enough copies to go round. The House of Lords – with its much smaller caseload – is much more efficient, but constitutionally outrageous. That's because in 1984 the Lords started charging the press and public for copies of their decisions (£4 a time or £200 for a year's season ticket). It's outrageous because, as we've said, the judgments are not read out; the House of Lords is the one court in the land whose decisions are available only to those who can afford to pay for them.

## The European Courts

People often talk about the European Court without realising there are two of them. Ask whether they mean the Strasbourg court or the Luxembourg court and they'll sheepishly admit they thought Strasbourg and Luxembourg were the same place really and located somewhere near The Hague. You of course (having read Chapter 1 of this book) will already know a little bit about the European Court of Human Rights in Strasbourg; all we propose here is to stress the main details. We'll then go on to look at the Luxembourg court.

### The European Court of Human Rights at Strasbourg

You have to begin a human rights case with the Commission – the

European Commission on Human Rights to give its full name. It has one member for each of the 21 countries in the Council of Europe; the British member is Sir Basil Hall, who was formerly the Treasury Solicitor. It doesn't meet continuously but there is of course a permanent staff to process applications. And these will only be considered by the Commission when you've exhausted all effective remedies in your own country – which often means that you've lost an appeal to the House of Lords. You've then got only six months to lodge your application in Strasbourg. Provided your application satisfies these conditions (and few do), the Commission will decide whether your application is admissible; the government you're suing may be asked for its comments and there may be a (private) oral hearing. If the application is admissible the Commission then tries to bring about what's called a 'friendly settlement' – banging heads together in slow motion by remote control from Strasbourg.

If there's no friendly settlement the Commission draws up an opinion on whether the Human Rights Convention has been violated. Like the mysterious Advocate-General's opinion which will be revealed in the next section, this is more like a judgment than an opinion – but it's not binding. It's sent to the committee of ministers, with a copy to the government involved – though not the applicant. The committee of ministers is really the committee of ministers' deputies, which means civil servants like Christopher Lush, the British Foreign Office official whose title is Ambassador and UK Permanent Representative to the Council of Europe. Many cases then get no further than that. The committee of ministers may decide against the case going on to the court (perhaps because the point raised is not of general legal importance) and the committee of ministers will then, in most cases, adopt the Commission's views on whether the Convention has been broken by the government concerned. But some cases – about a quarter of those declared admissible – do make it to the eighth square, and reach the European Court of Human Rights just across the lobby from the room where the Commission has met in secret conclave. Only the Commission or the government concerned has the power to refer the case to the court; strictly speaking the applicant has no right to appear before the court as it's the Commission's job to present all the arguments, but after a recent innovation applicants are now allowed to be represented before the court.

As with the Commission, the court has a judge for each country – our man is Sir Vincent Evans (who, like Christopher Lush, was once a legal adviser to the Foreign Office). When the Commission refers a case to the court it normally announces its opinion on it; although it sometimes refers important cases to the court where it thinks there's been no violation of the convention, the court tends not to disagree much with the Commission and so you can often make an informed guess about what the court will decide by looking at the Commission's report. Judgment is always reserved and tends to be a bit of an anti-climax – only two judges sit in a court designed to take twenty-one, and the parties involved in a case don't always bother to travel to Strasbourg to collect the printed text. The court has power to award damages and costs to the injured party. Of the 21 cases involving the United Kingdom which have been referred to the European Court, a breach of the Convention has been found in 12, and no breach in two. Seven were still pending when this book went to press. No other country has had so many cases referred, or so many violations established. But British ministers point out that Belgium, with a much smaller population, has a record which is nearly as bad; Britain has also allowed the right of individual petition to the court for longer than some other countries, such as France.

## The European Court of Justice at Luxembourg

The President of the European Court of Justice is now Lord MacKenzie Stuart (who, you will have gathered, is a Scottish judge); after more than 12 years in Luxembourg he's fed up with telling people that he doesn't work in Strasbourg (or Brussels, or The Hague) and that his court has nothing to do with Human Rights.

The best way to think of the European Court of Justice is as the Common Market court: its correct title is the Court of Justice of the European Communities. As you might expect, it's the court to which the twelve member countries and the Community institutions bring their disputes. But apart from these so-called Direct Actions it has another role of more direct relevance to people in Britain. Community law is part of our own law. Our own courts have to apply it. Sometimes that may cause them no problems. But if there's some dispute on how Community Law applies to a particular problem, any court or tribunal in Britain and the other Common Market countries can ask the Court of Justice in Luxembourg for an authoritative 'Preliminary Ruling'. This procedure is quite different from taking a case to the European Court of Human Rights at Strasbourg. That court will only take on a case when everything possible has already been done under the domestic law of the country involved. But the Luxembourg Court was perfectly happy to consider a case sent to them in 1983 by the Magistrates' Court at North Shields on Tyneside. They'd just fined the famous Captain Kent Kirk £30,000 for fishing inside Britain's 12-mile limit. But after the European Court had decided he was not breaking Community law, the Old Bailey in London quashed his conviction and gave him back the fine and costs. And a glance at the caseload of the European Court for 1985 will confirm the diversity of the United Kingdom courts which send cases on to it. They range from the Court of Appeal and the High Court to the Special Commissioners of Income Tax and the Belfast Industrial Tribunal.

At first sight the procedure of the European Court of Justice seems so strange to anyone brought up in the common law (rather than the Common Market) that you might wonder how it is that British lawyers were recently chosen for the top two jobs (President and Registrar). The answer that they stoutly maintain is that the procedure of the court is perfectly simple and straightforward. Even so, the Registrar, Paul Heim, has to resort to the example of Portia in *The Merchant of Venice* to explain the job of the strangely-named Advocate-General. It's Portia, you'll remember, who – dressed like a Doctor of Laws – offers to the Duke of Venice her opinion that Shylock is entitled to his pound of flesh but 'no jot of blood'. Portia here is more than an advocate – her opinion is really a judgment which in this case the Duke is more than happy

67

to accept. For 'Portia' substitute 'Advocate-General' and you begin to get an idea of what he (or she) does. The Advocate-General is neither an Advocate nor a General (just as the Lord Privy Seal is not a Lord, nor a performing seal, and certainly not a privy). He listens to the case along with the judges (though he sits to one side of the bench) and gives judgment on it before they do. His judgment is called an opinion and he delivers it standing up (whereas real judges the world over are allowed to speak from a sedentary position). But it's still a judgment and the Advocate-General has the same status (and high pay) as the judges he sits with.

The inconvenient thing about the judgment is that the Advocate-General's opinion is never the last word on the subject. That goes to the Court which – having read and discussed what the Advocate-General had to say about the case – can accept or reject the Advocate-General's arguments and conclusions. Clearly the Advocate-General's opinion offers the best available prediction of how the Court itself will eventually decide the case, but celebrations by a litigant who gets a favourable opinion from the Advocate-General may sometimes be premature. One can re-hearse the arguments in favour of keeping the Advocate-General, but in Luxembourg you may also hear the heretical suggestion that the Court would get through more cases a year if the Advocates-General were transformed into real judges – the sort who give their judgments sitting down.

## THE INTERNATIONAL COURT

There's yet another court based in Europe, the International Court of Justice at The Hague. This one is the United Nations court – it's also called, rather vaguely, The World Court. But before you get any grand ideas about taking your case there, we hasten to point out that only states can take proceedings. Individuals have often tried to petition the International Court; they have always failed to get a hearing (unless of course they could persuade a government to bring the case on their behalf).

The International Court decides disputes between states in accordance with international law. But this can only happen if the countries concerned have accepted the compulsory jurisdiction of the Court. Fewer than a third of the world's countries have done so. Of the five permanent members of the United Nations Security Council, only the United States and Britain accepted the Court's compulsory jurisdiction. Then the United States announced in October 1985 that it would no longer accept compulsory jurisdiction from April 1986 (because of a dispute with Nicaragua). The *Financial Times* columnist who writes under the name 'Justinian' said the US announcement was a 'blow to the development of an international legal order. It also confirms', he wrote, 'the waning respect for, and authority of, the court by the great powers and reflects the declining number of applications to the court during the last ten years.'

There are fifteen judges of the International Court. They are elected by the General Assembly and the Security Council; and they have diplomatic immunity. The British judge is Sir Robert Jennings.

## Legal Aid

Perhaps we should have put this section at the front of the book. After all, how many ordinary people can afford to go to court these days without legal aid paying at least something towards the lawyers' bills? In fact, as we explained on page 50, you may feel safe in making a small claim in the county court on your own – but it could still be worth your while seeing a solicitor under the Green Form Scheme before you start.

### The Green Form Scheme (Legal Advice)

Reassuringly, there really is a green form. You go to a solicitor, tell him (or her) about your savings and income, he (or she) fills in the green form, adds up the figures, and then tells you whether you qualify for what's called 'legal advice and assistance'. That phrase covers most legal problems such as divorce or maintenance, loss of your job, an accident, housing, landlord and tenant cases, hire-purchase problems and making a will. Under the Green Form Scheme a solicitor can give advice, write letters, take advice from a barrister, and prepare a written case if you have to go before a tribunal. It's on a fairly small scale; if the solicitor's fees are over £50 including cash he spends on your behalf, he may have to clear them with the Legal Aid Office.

When the scheme was set up in 1972 it was meant to cover everything but actually taking a case to court, but it's been extended to cover domestic proceedings in the magistrates' courts. This is called, rather pompously, 'assistance by way of representation'; it covers most civil cases handled by magistrates, such as maintenance, custody, affiliation, and defended adoption proceedings. But remember that magistrates can't grant divorces – to end a marriage you have to take proceedings in a county court. In fact, although legal aid is not normally available for undefended divorces, you can get free or cheap help from a solicitor with your divorce by seeing him under the Green Form Scheme and asking him for advice on how to conduct the divorce proceedings yourself. (The limit is then £90; after that the solicitor has to ask the Legal Aid Office for an extension.)

But are you likely to qualify for Legal Advice? If you're on supplementary benefit, or get family income supplement and don't have much in the way of savings, then the answer's easy – you'll get legal advice without even having to pay a contribution. If you're a little better off, it gets more complicated. As we've said, the solicitor will work out all the figures, but you may want a rough idea whether it's even worth asking him to do that. So here are the details – but here too is a word of warning. These figures took effect in November 1985 but there may have been changes since then. (You can get an up-to-date leaflet called *Legal Aid – Financial Limits* from The Law Society, who also publish a rather fuller *Legal Aid Guide*.)

To qualify under the Green Form Scheme, both your savings

and your income have to be within the limits. If you are married, your husband's or wife's savings and income will be included unless you live apart or it would be unfair to add them together. Your savings include any money, investments and valuable items of property. But you can leave out the value of the house you live in, your furniture, clothes, and the tools of your trade. If you have dependants (husband, wife, children, relatives) you can knock off £200 for one dependant, £320 for two and £60 each for any others. What's left is called your disposal capital. If it's more than £800, you can forget about the idea. If not, read on.

The next step is to work our your disposable income. Start with the money you've received over the past week (for example, your pay, pension, child benefit or whatever). Knock off the tax and national insurance contributions. Deduct £34.50 if you're living with your husband or wife; if you're separated or divorced you deduct the maintenance paid in the last seven days. Knock off £15.15 for a dependant child or relative under 11; £22.65 for one between 11 and 15; £27.30 for one aged 16 or 17; and £35.40 for one over 18. What's left? If it's less than £54 you get legal advice free. If it's more than £114 then again you can forget it. If it's between those two figures you may have to contribute towards the cost of the advice. The size of the contribution depends on how big your disposable weekly income is, but it ranges from £5 (for people who have between £54 and £62 a week) to £62 (for people who've got between £108 and £114 a week left after making these deductions).

So far so good. Now here's the snag. Let's say you've qualified under the scheme (perhaps with a contribution) and you win your case. Where property is recovered (or even just preserved) under the Green Form Scheme, your solicitor will use it to pay his bill. You only get what's left. The rule does not apply if it would cause you great hardship or distress, or if it would be difficult to enforce because of the kind of property recovered; or in certain matrimonial or benefit cases. But when it does apply, you may well feel you've wasted your time – and the only person who's got anything out of it is the solicitor. He has what's called a 'statutory charge' over the money recovered. After he's taken his costs out of your winnings there may be nothing left. In fact, there could be less than nothing because you might have had to pay a contribution to his fees as well. So beware. Once your solicitor has finished filling in your Green Form with the help of his pocket calculator and strange bits of cardboard, he'll probably be able to tell you straight away whether you're eligible for legal advice. The first piece of advice you should ask for is what effect the statutory charge might have in your case.

## Civil Legal Aid

As we've said, Legal Advice under the Green Form Scheme covers everything but litigation (with the exception of non-criminal Magistrates' Court work). 'Civil Legal Aid' covers non-criminal court proceedings themselves. You may already have had advice under the Green Form Scheme if you've been trying to get your opponent to settle without going to court. On the other hand it might be worth trying to get Legal Aid even if you were rejected under the Green Form Scheme, because Legal Aid is available even if your savings are a good bit higher than the top figure for Legal Advice.

Civil Legal Aid is not available for proceedings before most tribunals (apart from the Employment Appeal Tribunal). It's also not available in the coroner's court or for libel cases. And because much larger sums of money are usually involved, the procedure is more complicated than for Legal Advice under the Green Form Scheme.

First, the money side. It's not your solicitor who works out whether your income and savings are within the limits – it's the Department of Health and Social Security. You will have to fill in a form sent to you by post and give them all your financial details. Your husband's or wife's income and savings will be added to yours unless you live apart or if there's a conflict of interest – such as in a divorce case. This, as you can imagine, all takes time – months in fact – although your solicitor can apply for Emergency Legal Aid by telephone if it's essential. To get Legal Aid your disposable capital has to be worked out in the same way as it would if you wanted Legal Advice under the Green Form Scheme. But you can have savings up to £3,000 without having to pay a contribution. If your disposable capital is more than £4,710, Legal Aid will only be granted in exceptional cases where the costs are likely to be very high. Between those two figures you'll have to pay a contribution. This could be the whole amount you have over £3,000 – though to begin with, you probably won't be asked for more than the estimated costs of your case.

You also have to qualify on annual income. The DHSS will estimate your income for the next year and deduct rent, rates, income tax, maintenance of your dependents, and other necessary outgoings. Under £2,255 you get free legal aid. Up to £5,415 you have to pay a contribution of up to a quarter of the income over that figure. Over £5,415 and you'll be turned down.

But that's still only half the battle. If the DHSS decides you're eligible (with or without a contribution) the Legal Aid Office then has to decide whether you have reasonable grounds for going to court. They consider the facts of the case and what the law says (they may allow you to get a barrister's opinion which will help you and them to see how strong your case is) and they'll only grant you Legal Aid if they think it's reasonable to do so.

If you satisfy both the DHSS and the Legal Aid Office (which, in a curious way, is run by The Law Society but paid for by the Lord Chancellor's Department) then you'll either get a free Legal Aid Certificate or an offer of a certificate subject to a contribution from savings, or income (or both). You can then decide whether or not to accept the offer, pay the first contribution, and get the certificate. That's when the solicitor starts work on the case.

The stakes are higher than under the Green Form Scheme (which normally covers a much lower figure than a Legal Aid Certificate). So too is the sum you might lose under the statutory charge we mentioned earlier. Of course if you win your case and the other side pays all your costs, you should get your contribution back. If you lose, you may have to pay part or all of your opponent's costs as well as your contribution. But even if you win your case and don't get all your costs paid by the other side, then you'll find the statutory charge will drop like a guillotine. The

Legal Aid fund takes its money out of your winnings – and the costs can be considerable. The problem is particularly acute when a husband and wife – perhaps both on legal aid – are getting divorced and fighting over the children or who's to get the house. If it has to be sold, then the Legal Aid fund will generally take its share of the proceeds to cover the costs – which may not leave the former spouses with as much as they were expecting to live on. We repeat: beware the statutory charge. Don't assume that Legal Aid gives you something for nothing. Don't apply for Legal Aid unless you know what you stand to lose.

## Criminal Legal Aid

So far we've been talking about Legal Advice and Legal Aid which are run by The Law Society under the general guidance of the Lord Chancellor. 'Criminal Legal Aid' is nothing to do with The Law Society; it's the direct responsibility of the Lord Chancellor's Department.

If you are charged with a criminal offence you should ask the court straight away for legal aid (unless you are sure you won't qualify). The court will decide whether it's in the interests of justice for you to have legal representation in court. This means you can expect to get Criminal Legal Aid if you're in real danger of going to prison or losing your reputation or job; or if there are difficult legal questions to be answered – which covers virtually all Crown Court trials. The court will also decide whether you need Criminal Legal Aid on financial grounds. You won't be refused Criminal Legal Aid for financial reasons if you are on supplementary benefit. Again, if you're on Family Income Supplement, only the size of your savings can disqualify you from free legal aid. Otherwise it's a case of working out your disposable capital and disposable income in more or less the same way as for Civil Legal Aid. If your disposable capital is more than £3,000 you can be ordered to make a contribution towards your Criminal Legal Aid of any money you have over that sum. If your average disposable weekly income is £46 or more, you may again have to contribute about a quarter of the amount you earn over that sum. You may have to make a contribution towards legal aid even if you are acquitted.

We warned you earlier about the risks of the statutory charge if you apply for Civil Legal Aid. This does not apply in criminal cases; and while you can decide whether it's worth your while to bring a civil case, you've got no choice if you're being prosecuted for a criminal offence. So don't hesitate to apply for Criminal Legal Aid if you need it – it may not be free, but it generally won't be as expensive as paying a solicitor privately. (This advice does not apply to the more 'successful' type of criminal for whom money, as a result of his success, is no object.)

## Duty solicitors

If you've been charged with a criminal offence but don't have Criminal Legal Aid or Legal Advice under the Green Form Scheme, then you may find there's a 'duty solicitor' at the Magistrates' Court who will advise you and represent you at the hearing. The duty solicitor claims his fees direct from the Legal Aid Fund. This scheme was introduced by the Legal Aid Act 1982. It was extended by the Police and Criminal Evidence Act 1984 to cover advice by duty solicitors at police stations.

As you'll see in the next chapter, the 1984 Act gives people interviewed at police stations the right to see a solicitor (subject to certain conditions). If you're arrested – and even if you assist the police voluntarily – you may not know a solicitor who's prepared to come to the station while you're being questioned, and it was for this reason that provision was made for solicitors to be on call, ready to visit police stations at any time. The new service is free, with no means test.

But at the beginning of 1986 the Law Society estimated that only just over half of England and Wales was covered by the 24-hour scheme. Only about ten per cent of London north of the Thames was covered, compared with total coverage in parts of the West Midlands and the North West.

The government announced in the summer of 1985 that there would be two levels of advice under the new scheme. If you're being questioned about an arrestable offence (in general, one for which you can get 5 years in prison), the amount of time a solicitor can spend in the police station is unlimited. For other offences the maximum pay a solicitor can claim from the Legal Aid Fund is £50 – which effectively limits him to about two hours including his travelling time on each case. That's because, under Legal Aid, solicitors get £27 an hour for work done at the police station and for time spent travelling or waiting; duty solicitors get £36 an hour but only when working out of office hours for people charged with an arrestable offence.

Reacting to the scheme, two leading solicitors with criminal practices said the 'feeling of disaffection amongst London practitioners at the attitude of a recalcitrant government is profound'. Some London solicitors predicted a boycott of the scheme in an attempt to persuade the government to abolish the limits on non-arrestable offences. Others felt it was their duty to try to make a go of it.

A hurried experiment was held in South London which showed a surprisingly low take-up of the free legal advice on offer at police stations – on average 13% of people arrested asked for legal advice at some time while in police custody. During the two-week experiment there were only 19 calls to the special duty solicitor telephone referral service from the five police stations involved. The Law Society's report on the experiment found, however, 'circumstantial evidence that the procedures . . . set out in the code of practice were not consistently followed by the police'. But the report also explained that the experiment had been set up at short notice and some police officers may not have realised exactly how the system was meant to work. (Incidentally, the plan is that the duty solicitor's phone number will only be known by the police.) The message, though, is clear. You have a right to legal advice at a police station – even if you've not actually been arrested. If you don't have a solicitor of your own, ask for the duty solicitor. You may have to wait for him. He may only be able to spend a little time with you – perhaps he'll only speak to you on the telephone. In some parts of the country he may not come at all. But – if you can – use your rights.

## The European Courts

Both the European Courts (though not of course the International Court) grant a form of legal aid. In Human Rights cases you or your solicitor should apply direct to Strasbourg; the Legal Aid Offices in Britain won't be able to help. For Luxembourg cases the position is more complicated.

If you want to go to the European Court of Human Rights in Strasbourg, you'll have to begin, as we've explained, at the European Commission of Human Rights. The Commission says it has funds which enable it 'in certain circumstances, to grant free legal aid to an applicant of limited means. . . . The applicant must prove his lack of means by producing an officially certified document.' Although individuals don't have the right to appear before the European Court of Human Rights, they may 'express the wish to take part in the proceedings'. In that case, you must be represented by a lawyer. If you've been granted legal aid before the Commission, the grant continues in force before the court. 'Otherwise', in the words of an official guide, 'the President of the Court may, under certain conditions, at any time grant legal aid at the applicant's request'.

The European Court of Justice in Luxembourg can also grant legal aid. The applicant must provide 'supporting evidence' and the court decides whether it would be in the interests of justice to grant it. This applies in 'direct actions', such as the one Stanley Adams won against the European Commission which had disclosed to his former employers that he was a 'whistle-blower'. But as we've said, you're more likely to come across the Luxembourg Court when a national court asks it for a preliminary ruling on Community Law. Since this is regarded as a step in proceedings before a national court, it ought to be possible to get your Legal Aid – whether Criminal or Civil – extended to Luxembourg. But if this fails, or if Legal Aid was not available in the national court, you can apply to the European Court, which has funds 'in special circumstances, to assist the representation and attendance of a party'.

# JURIES

## The Lamp of Freedom

Lord Devlin said in his famous Hamlyn lectures in 1956 that trial by jury is a protection against tyranny: it gives protection against laws which the ordinary man may regard as harsh and oppressive. In a passage that has often been quoted, Lord Devlin maintained that no tyrant could afford to leave a subject's freedom in the hands of twelve of his countrymen: 'trial by jury is more than an instrument of justice and more than one wheel of the constitution,' said Lord Devlin; 'it is the lamp that shows that freedom lives.'

But while tyrants are fairly rare in our recent history, what Lord Devlin called 'harsh and oppressive laws' are far from unknown. For Lord Devlin, the jury is an insurance that the criminal law will conform to the ordinary man's idea of what is fair and just. If it does not, the jury will not be a party to its enforcement. Lord Devlin said there was no use in Parliament making laws which would not be enforced. MPs might put it down to the perversity of juries, but in Lord Devlin's view, 'if there is a law which the juryman constantly shows by his verdicts that he dislikes, it is worth examining the law to see if there is anything wrong with it, rather than the juryman'.

John Mathew QC, interviewed on the BBC Radio 4 programme *Law in Action* in July 1985, gave some examples of this: 'a century or two ago,' he said, 'when sheep stealing was a capital offence, juries started to refuse to convict for that very reason and that led to a change in the law. Nowadays juries who disbelieve police officers – even where there may be other, possibly sufficient, evidence to convict – will acquit in order to demonstrate that they do not approve.'

The former New York judge Marvin E. Frankel said on the same programme that there were times when this 'rough justice' was a defect in the system rather than a virtue. 'For example,' the judge said, 'we had a whole era in the Southern part of the United States when sheriffs and other public officials clearly guilty of

78

lynching and other crimes of violence against black citizens were routinely acquitted by juries because of local prejudice.'

In everyone's minds at that recording was a case earlier in 1985 where many people thought that a jury had refused to convict because it disapproved of the law. What went on in the minds of the jurors who acquitted Clive Ponting on secrets charges we shall probably never know, because section 8 of the Contempt of Court Act 1981 makes it an offence for a journalist to ask them what was said in the jury room. (But it's not illegal to ask jurors about the desirability of bringing the prosecution or what they thought of the judge or the barristers.)

However, Clive Ponting himself says in his book *The Right to Know* that he had to face a vetted jury, part of the trial *in camera* and a summing up by the judge that left him with no legal defence. 'Yet despite all of this,' writes Clive Ponting, 'I was acquitted, probably because the jury did not like the way in which the judge had interpreted "the interests of the state" as being the same as "the political interests of the Government". This', he says, 'was widely seen as victory for commonsense and a blow for democracy by the jury.'

## Jury vetting

As Clive Ponting said, it was a vetted jury that acquitted him. A panel of nearly sixty Londoners were vetted to ensure there would be enough potential jurors available. In 1980 Sir Michael Havers, the Attorney General, had made a statement in the House of Commons on 'jury checks', as he called them. He explained that they involved checking police special branch records, and his permission was required for this to be done. 'Except in terrorist cases,' said the Attorney General, 'such checks will not be authorised in cases involving so-called strong political motives. In cases involving security, such as under the Official Secrets Act, such checks will be authorised only when national security is involved and it is expected that the court will be asked to sit in camera.' In no other type of case would such checks be authorised. The Attorney added that as all parties to the proceedings have a statutory right under the Juries Act 1974 to inspect the jury panel, the judge's authority for police access to the names was not needed. But, he said, the judge and defence counsel would be informed when a check had been authorised.

The Attorney General's guidelines, issued at the same time as his statement, explained that the special branch were asked whether a potential juror was known for what the guidelines describe as 'political beliefs . . . so biased as to go beyond normally reflecting the broad spectrum of views and interests of the community . . . to a degree which might interfere with his fair assessment of the facts of the case or lead him to exert improper pressure on his fellow jurors'.

Lord Silkin, who as Sam Silkin was Attorney General in the Labour Government of 1974–1979, wrote in *The Observer* in 1979 that jury vetting had been going on for at least 30 years – and probably much longer. In 1974 he and the then Home Secretary Roy Jenkins decided the practice should continue, subject to rigid controls. 'We agreed', he said, 'that to forbid it altogether could open the way to the fear of corruption, intimidation and even worse in certain very limited classes of cases where the defendants, or their enemies, might stop at nothing to achieve an acquittal or a conviction.' The main objection to jury vetting, according to Lord Silkin, is that it conflicts with the random selection of jurors. But, he said, random selection was limited by the right of both prosecution and defence to remove jurors in court.

## Challenging jurors

A defendant is allowed three 'peremptory challenges': he can challenge up to three would-be jurors without giving any reason. Each defendant can use his three challenges, which means that if there are several people in the dock their counsel may well be able to affect the composition of the jury. But all the defendants really have to go on is the juror's appearance – whether the person who's about to take the oath is male or female, young or old, black or white, scruffy or respectable, establishment or liberated.

And the challenge can't be made after the juror has taken the oath, which means defence counsel can't take into account the juror's accent (he might be from the same part of the United Kingdom as the defendant) or his level of education. In fact some people found the jury oath so hard to read out that the wording was simplified at the end of 1984. It now reads, 'I swear by Almighty God that I will faithfully try the defendant and give a true verdict according to the evidence'.

The prosecution also have the right to challenge without cause, asking would-be jurors to 'stand by for the Crown', which means they go to the back of the queue and are not called.

Both the prosecution and the defence have the right to challenge 'for cause'. According to Lord Devlin in his lectures on trial by jury, 'a challenge for cause means that the party challenging must, if he is to succeed, show either that the juror challenged is not qualified to serve on the jury or else that he is biased or has a discreditable character'. This procedure is known as the *voir dire*, a phrase not heard in England because the challenge for cause is extremely rare here. John Mathew QC and Sir David Napley say in a paper prepared for the American Bar Association's Conference in London in 1985 that a prima facie case must be established before a potential juror can be cross-examined. 'Probably the last occasion on which this was done', they write, 'was at the Central Criminal Court in 1969 during the Kray Trial, when jurors were allowed to be cross-examined as to whether they had read and been influenced by certain prejudicial newspaper reports. In the trial of Jeremy Thorpe, as an alternative to permitting jurors to be questioned, the judge himself, at the invitation of the defence, enquired of the jurors whether they had read a book by two journalists which had been an initiating factor in the launching of the prosecution.'

In the United States, of course, the *voir dire* is far from rare. Judge Marvin Frankel, in his paper to the American Bar Association Conference, says the random selection of a potential jury panel for the particular case is, for the American lawyer, a step closer to the beginning of the process rather than its probable end. 'The actual breadth and form of the inquiry permitted by the court varies with the case and place, and may consume hours, days, or weeks.' On *Law in Action* Judge Frankel said the *voir dire* system tends to be 'misused to cosy up the jury and predispose members of the jury to a particular point of view, rather than to smoke out improper biases or prejudices. Many people', he said, 'believe the procedure is abused, that it is wasteful, that it does not repay the effort, that the expense is unwarranted and that the burden on people called for jury service is unwarranted.' However, he conceded that change was unlikely in the foreseeable future.

One should not be too smug about not using challenges for cause in England. We manage to avoid them because we believe the restrictions on what may be published about a case before the trial means that jurors arrive at court in a state of blissful ignorance. Americans would never accept such restrictions on freedom of information as are thought necessary here.

Incidentally the fact that some jurors will be challenged means that a prudent court will always have more potential jurors on the premises than are likely to be needed. This means that if you are called for jury service you will probably spend a lot of time hanging around and doing nothing. Even if you have a case there are often legal arguments about the evidence which take place with the jury out. So take a good book to read. If you flash this one around, you'll probably be seen as a know-all, or a clever-dick, and elected foreman. Come to think of it, if you flash any sort of book around you'll probably get the job.

## Who can serve?

Before 1973 there was a property qualification for service on a jury; now, anyone between 18 and 65 on the electoral register is liable to be called. But some people are ineligible, presumably because they know too much about the system: they include judges, magistrates, lawyers, the police, prison officers, probation officers, and clergymen. Others are disqualified because they know too much about the system from the other end: under the Juries (Disqualification) Act 1984 anyone who has served any period of imprisonment during the previous ten years is disqualified. So too is anyone who has received a suspended sentence or has had a community service order imposed during the previous ten years, and anyone placed on probation during the previous five years. Anyone sentenced to five years or more imprisonment is disqualified for life.

There are a number of people who can ask to be excused jury service: members of Parliament, the armed forces, and the medical profession, for example; and others who would suffer great hardship if they had to give up their time. If you get a jury summons, and it's difficult to serve at the time you've been called, it's always worth writing back to the jury summoning officer to explain the circumstances. But don't ignore it or you can be fined £100 under the Juries Act 1974.

A similar penalty can be imposed on a juror who turns up in court but is not available when called on to serve, or who is unfit for service by reason of drink or drugs. It is a contempt of court for a juror to leave the court without permission; and jurors can also be fined for misbehaviour. (Wearing a horror mask as he was about to be sworn in cost one would-be juror £50 in 1979.) It used to be the case that the jury were kept locked up without 'meat, drink, fire or candle' until they reached a verdict, and in 1578 a juror was fined twenty shillings for having with him a box of 'preserved sweetmeats, sugar-candy and liquorice'. Nowadays when even judges chew peppermints in court, it's unlikely that eating sweets would be punishable as contempt.

## Fraud trials and the Roskill Committee

In 1983, a senior judge called for reforms in the way commercial fraud trials were dealt with. He said they were unfair on the accused, the barristers, the judge, and the jury; and he suggested alternative ways in which these cases could be heard without randomly-selected jurors.

That judge was Lord Roskill, and when he was appointed a few months later to see what changes in fraud trials would be desirable for the 'just, expeditious and economical disposal of such proceedings', there were people who thought the committee had been set up by the government in the expectation that it would recommend the abolition of juries in serious fraud trials. And after that, why stop at fraud?

Certainly the government was against keeping juries in fraud trials. The Director of Public Prosecutions, Sir Thomas Hetherington, whose views in this case reflected those of the Attorney General, Sir Michael Havers, believed there was a strong argument in relation to a very limited group of complicated fraud cases for having a judge sitting with assessors rather than with a jury.

Lord Roskill's report was published in January 1986. By a majority of seven to one, the committee recommended that 'complex' fraud cases should be tried by a judge sitting with two handpicked laymen instead of by a judge and jury. The government immediately welcomed the report and made it clear that at least some of Lord Roskill's hundred recommendations would be included in a Criminal Justice Bill at the end of 1986. Whether the plan to drop jury trial in some cases would be included in the bill had not been decided when we went to press.

Lord Roskill also recommended that the right of peremptory challenge (see page 80) should be abolished in fraud trials; if the government decided to accept the view of those who claimed late in 1985 that this right was being abused, it was thought likely peremptory challenge would be abolished or restricted in all trials, not just those for fraud.

# 3 Civil liberties

## THE POLICE AND CRIMINAL EVIDENCE ACT 1984

In a speech made a couple of days after the Police and Criminal Evidence Act finally completed its long and difficult passage through Parliament, the then Home Secretary Mr Leon Brittan described it as 'both a law and order, and civil liberties measure. As such,' he said, 'it will provide the framework for modern policing with consent into the twenty-first century.' In the same speech Mr Brittan made it clear that the main provisions of the Act were likely to take effect from the beginning of January 1986. What follows now is only an outline of that framework. If you want to read the fine print, we suggest either the book on the Act written by Fiona Hargreaves and Howard Levenson (published by Legal Action Group and comprehensive, though very hard to read because of the authors' obsession with 'him/her', 'his/her', and – worst of all – 's/he') or Michael Zander's book (published by Sweet and Maxwell and written by an author who, in his own words, participated 'in this great and continuing debate' – though he says he tried not to allow his personal views on the legislation to intrude).

### Powers to stop and search

Section 1 of the Act allows a police officer to stop and search any person or vehicle for stolen or 'prohibited' articles. A prohibited article is an offensive weapon, or an implement used in connection with various types of theft. If the policeman does find articles which he reasonably suspects are stolen or prohibited, he can seize them. The police are only allowed to stop people in public areas – not in their own homes. And, most important of all, a policeman is only allowed to search a person or vehicle if he has reasonable grounds for suspecting he will find stolen or prohibited articles.

An unusual feature of this Act is that the Home Secretary has had to issue four so-called codes of practice. These remind the police of the powers they've been given and tell them how the powers are to be used. A police officer who fails to observe the codes is liable to disciplinary proceedings, and the breach – though not in itself against the law – can be taken into account when the case comes to court. The codes also include what are called 'notes for guidance', but as these are not considered part of the codes they can presumably be ignored by the police without the risk that disciplinary proceedings will follow.

The code of practice on Stop and Search makes it clear that reasonable suspicion lies somewhere between a hunch or instinct on the one hand and certainty or near-certainty on the other. 'There must be some concrete basis for the officer's suspicion . . . which can be considered and evaluated by an objective third person.' In a clear reference to black people who claim they are stopped simply because they are black, the code says, 'a person's colour of itself can never be a reasonable ground for suspicion. The mere fact alone that a person is carrying a particular kind of property or is dressed in a certain way or has a certain hairstyle is likewise not of itself sufficient.' And the note for guidance advises the police to use the powers of stop and search 'responsibly and sparingly' to avoid 'mistrust of the police among sections of the community'.

Section 2 of the Act introduces a number of safeguards. The policeman must take reasonable steps to give his name, the name of his police station, the object of his search and his ground for making it; he must tell the person being searched that he's normally entitled to a copy of the officer's written record of the search. The policeman has no power to make a person take off any of his clothes in public apart from an outer coat, jacket or gloves, though there's nothing to stop him asking. The code of practice says every reasonable effort must be made to reduce to the minimum the embarrassment a person being searched may feel, although reasonable force may be used as a last resort. Any search involving the removal of more than outer clothing must be done in private with nobody from the opposite sex present.

Section 4 of the Act allows the police to set up road blocks to see whether a vehicle is carrying an escaped prisoner or somebody involved in a serious arrestable offence. The person being sought may have committed the offence, or witnessed it, or be intending to commit such an offence in the future. What then is a 'serious arrestable offence'?

This is an important question, because the phrase is used throughout the Act. First of all, you have to decide whether the crime is an arrestable offence (without the 'serious'). An arrestable offence is one for which you can get five years in prison. So too are certain other specified offences – for example all offences under the Official Secrets Act. The arrestable offence will then be 'serious' if it has led to certain consequences, or if it's intended or likely to lead to those consequences. The consequences are serious harm to security of the state or public order; serious interference with the administration of justice or the investigation of offences; death; serious injury; substantial financial gain; or financial loss which is serious to the person who suffers it. Moreover, some arrestable offences are always considered serious, even if none of these consequences applies. Crimes which are always serious arrestable offences include treason; murder; manslaughter; rape; kidnapping; intercourse with a girl under 13; buggery with a boy under 16 or anyone who has not consented; indecent assault amounting to gross indecency; causing an explosion likely to endanger life or property; certain firearms offences; causing death by reckless driving; hostage-taking; and hi-jacking.

## Powers of entry, search and seizure

Section 8 of the Act allows a magistrate to grant a search warrant authorising the police to enter and search premises. The magistrate must be satisfied that there are reasonable grounds for believing a serious arrestable offence (as defined in the previous section) has been committed. The magistrate must also be satisfied there are reasonable grounds for believing there is material on the premises which is likely to be of substantial value to the investigation of the offence. And there must be reasonable grounds for believing either that it's not practicable to communicate with anyone entitled to let the police in; or that it's not practicable to communicate with anyone entitled to grant access to the evidence; or that entry will be refused; or that the evidence will vanish unless the police get in quickly. But inevitably there are exceptions. The warrant can't be issued if the evidence includes 'items subject to legal privilege'; or 'excluded material'; or 'special procedure material'.

'Items subject to legal privilege' include communications between a lawyer and his client relating to legal advice or legal proceedings.

'Excluded material' includes personal records held in confidence and journalistic material held in confidence. The definitions in the Act go into more detail but in due course the courts will have to decide precisely what these phrases cover. It is not very helpful to be told by the Act that ' "journalistic material" means material acquired or created for the purposes of journalism'.

'Special procedure material' includes evidence held on a confidential basis (other than 'personal records') and journalistic material which is not held in confidence.

'Personal records' are documents which relate to the health or welfare of an identifiable individual.

As we've just said, a magistrate can't issue a search warrant for items subject to legal privilege, or excluded material, or special procedure material. In fact, nobody can authorise the police to search for items subject to legal privilege. The other two categories are different.

The police can get access to excluded material or special procedure material by applying to a circuit judge for a 'production order'. Certain conditions must be met, depending on which sort of material is being sought. The person who has the material must be given notice of the application. If the application is successful the judge will order the person who has the material to allow the police to look at it or take it away. Refusal is a contempt of court. Access to special procedure material is only allowed if this would be in the public interest. In addition to these powers to make production orders, the circuit judge is also allowed to issue a search warrant in certain cases.

There is also a detailed Code of Practice on search and seizure. It says, for example, that 'searches must be conducted with due consideration for the property and privacy of the occupier of the premises searched, and with no more disturbance than necessary'. The general message behind the code seems to be that the police should behave reasonably: they should do no more than they have to, but if they really do have to use their powers then the powers are there to be used.

Section 17 of the Act allows the police to enter and search premises, without a search warrant, to arrest someone for an arrestable offence or certain other offences; or to recapture an escaped prisoner; or to save life or limb or prevent serious damage to property. If the policeman is trying to arrest somebody under these powers he must have reasonable grounds for believing the person he's looking for is on the premises. There are also powers under section 18 allowing the police to search premises occupied or controlled by someone they've arrested.

Section 19 gives a policeman who's lawfully on the premises power to seize certain items. He can seize anything there he reasonably believes has been obtained as a consequence of an offence, or is evidence of an offence, so long as he reasonably believes it's necessary to seize the items or evidence to prevent it being concealed, lost, damaged, altered or destroyed. There is an exception for items subject to legal privilege (see above, page 88).

## Arrest

We've explained earlier in this chapter that an 'arrestable offence' is generally one for which you can get five years in prison; there are other arrestable offences defined in section 24 of the Act. Anybody may arrest somebody who's in the act of committing an arrestable offence, or who the person doing the arresting reasonably suspects is committing the offence. And if an arrestable offence has already been committed, anybody may arrest somebody who is guilty of it, or reasonably suspected to be guilty of it. What this means is that if the court decides later that no offence was committed by the arrested person, or by anyone else, the arrest will have been unlawful unless the person doing the arresting can show he reasonably suspected the other person was in the act of committing the offence.

So far we've been talking about what is sometimes called 'citizen's arrest'. The police, of course, have greater powers. For them to arrest lawfully someone reasonably suspected of having committed an arrestable offence, there's no need for an offence to have been committed, so long as the police reasonably suspect the possible or contemplated commission of an offence. And they can also arrest anyone they reasonably suspect is about to commit an offence.

Section 25 goes much further. It gives the police powers to arrest people in certain circumstances even if the offence is not 'arrestable'. (You'll remember that, broadly speaking, an arrestable offence is one for which you can get five years in prison.) Where the officer reasonably suspects that a non-arrestable offence has been committed or attemped, or is being committed or attempted, he may arrest anyone he reasonably suspects has done it, or tried it, or is doing it, if he thinks that for certain reasons it's impracticable or inappropriate to serve that person with a summons later on to appear in court. These reasons are called the 'general arrest conditions'. The first is that the constable doesn't know and can't readily find out the name of the person involved. Another justification for the arrest would be where the constable reasonably thinks he's been given a false name. The next general arrest condition applies where the person involved has failed to provide an address for service of the summons (not necessarily a home address), or where the constable reasonably doubts the address is satisfactory for service.

The remaining conditions relate to the inappropriateness of serving a summons later. The constable can carry out an arrest if he reasonably believes it's necessary to prevent the arrested person injuring himself (or someone else); being injured; causing loss or damage to property; committing an offence against public decency where there are people around; or obstructing the highway. An arrest is also possible if the constable reasonably believes it's necessary to protect a child or 'other vulnerable person'.

Section 28 says a person who is arrested must be told the grounds of arrest at the time he's arrested, or as soon as practicable afterwards. A person who's managed to escape before being given the reason for his arrest is unlikely to come to a police station and complain, but just in case the section prudently absolves the police in such cases.

Section 29 makes clear what people 'helping police with their enquiries' don't always understand – if you're not arrested you don't have to stay at a police station, and if the police want you to stay against your wishes they must arrest you and tell you at once.

## Detention

The next part of the Act tells the police when they can detain you at a police station. The police must appoint 'custody officers' at designated stations – those large enough to hold people who've been arrested. It's the job of the custody officer to make sure people in police detention are treated in accordance with the Act and the code of conduct; he also has to keep records. In principle the custody officer should not be the officer investigating the offence for which the detained person is in custody.

Section 37 says the custody officer must decide whether he has enough evidence to charge the person who's been arrested. He can detain the person while he decides this but must make his decision 'as soon as practicable'. If there's not enough evidence the detained person must be released, unless the custody officer reasonably believes continued detention is necessary to get evidence, by questioning him or otherwise. This legalises detention for questioning, but the questioning must be about the offence for which the person detained has been arrested; there is no power to arrest just for questioning.

If there is enough evidence, the arrested person must be charged or released. If he's charged, he must then be released unless certain conditions apply. The first justification for keeping a person in custody after he's been charged is that he seems not to have provided his real name or address. The second applies where

91

detention is necessary for his own protection; or to prevent him injuring somebody or damaging property. The third justification for holding somebody applies where the custody officer reasonably believes the person arrested will fail to appear in court or will interfere with the administration of justice. A juvenile (under 17) can also be detained if the custody officer reasonably believes it's in the juvenile's own interests.

The need for a person to remain in police detention must be reviewed by the police after six hours and then every nine hours after that, subject to certain exceptions.

If an arrested person is not charged, he can only be kept in police detention for a limited period. The clock normally starts running when he arrives at the police station. If he's arrested at a police station, the time is calculated from the moment of arrest. As a rule the maximum period is 24 hours; a person who has not been charged within that period must then be released. He can't be rearrested without a warrant for the same offence unless there's new evidence.

Detention without charge may be extended by 12 hours to 36 hours in certain circumstances. A senior officer must reasonably believe that investigation of a serious arrestable offence is being conducted expeditiously and the continued detention is necessary to secure, preserve or obtain evidence. There are various safeguards.

Further detention can be authorised by a Magistrates' Court for the same reasons. The detained person must be brought to court and is entitled to be legally represented. The magistrates – who sit in private – can authorise further detention for any further period of up to 36 hours – in other words 72 hours after the clock started running.

If further detention has been authorised, the police can ask the court to extend it; again for the same reasons and subject to the same safeguards. The longest period for which somebody can be detained without charge is 96 hours from when the clock started running – 4 days. But this is to be interpreted 'approximately'.

So far we've been talking about detention without charge.

Section 46 says somebody who has been charged should be brought before a Magistrates' Court on the day he's charged or the day afterwards (unless it's a Saturday).

Taking into account the fact that if a person is arrested in a different police area the police are allowed up to 24 hours to bring him to the appropriate station for questioning before the clock even begins to run, Fiona Hargreaves and Howard Levenson have calculated that someone arrested just after midnight on a Monday morning may not appear in a public court until, say, 4 pm the following Monday – after the best part of eight days in police detention.

## Questioning and treatment by police

Section 54 allows the police to search anyone at a police station who has been arrested if the custody officer thinks this is necessary to enable him to compile a list of the arrested person's property. The police can keep an arrested person's clothes if they believe he may use them to hurt himself.

Section 55 authorises what are known as 'intimate searches'. These involve physical examination of a person's body orifices for concealed items. They can be authorised by a senior officer who reasonably believes an arrested person has a weapon or a Class A drug concealed inside his body. Only doctors or nurses are allowed to fish around inside somebody else's body for drugs. If it's not practicable for a doctor or nurse to search for concealed weapons, a police officer of the same sex is allowed to do the job. Reasonable force may be used if necessary.

Section 56 says that a person who has been arrested and is being held by the police is entitled to have someone told as soon as practicable. A senior officer can delay this for up to 36 hours if the person has been arrested for a serious arrestable offence and the officer reasonably believes that passing on details of the arrest will alert other people suspected of a serious arrestable offence or lead to interference with evidence. There are various safeguards in the Code of Conduct.

Under section 58 a person is entitled to consult a solicitor privately as soon as practicable. Again a senior officer can delay this for up to 36 hours in the circumstances listed in the last paragraph. For details of the Duty Solicitor Scheme, which is designed to provide free legal advice 24 hours a day to anyone detained at a police station, see page 75.

Section 61 allows a senior police officer (superintendent or above) to take the fingerprints of someone detained at a police station without his consent if the officer reasonably suspects that the person is involved in any criminal offence and that taking prints will tend to confirm or disprove his involvement. Once someone has been charged with an offence recordable in national police records his fingerprints may be taken compulsorily without the need for authorisation by the senior officer.

We managed to mention intimate searches a little while ago without listing all the body orifices where people sometimes hide things (incidentally, ears and mouths are included). We must now talk of 'intimate samples' which are defined in the Act: they include a sample of blood, semen or any other tissue fluid, urine, saliva or pubic hair, or a swab taken from a person's body orifice. These are contrasted with non-intimate samples – hair other than pubic hair, a sample taken from a nail or from under a nail, a swab taken from any part of a person's body other than a body orifice, and a footprint. Intimate samples may only be taken from a person in police custody if he consents in writing. In addition, the sample must be authorised by a senior officer who reasonably believes the sample will tend to confirm or disprove the person's involvement in a serious arrestable offence. Refusal may be taken into account by a jury as corroborative evidence. Non-intimate samples may be taken without consent with the authority of a senior officer in the way just mentioned. Reasonable force may be used.

## Complaints against the police

Section 83 of the Police and Criminal Evidence Act established the Police Complaints Authority, which replaced the Police Complaints Board in April 1985. Its Chairman is Sir Cecil Clothier, the former Ombudsman. There are two deputy chairmen, and nine other members. All work full time. No former or serving police officer is eligible for membership of the Board. The address of the Police Complaints Authority is 10 Great George Street, London SW1P 3AE.

The Police Complaints Authority employs no investigators of its own; that job is left to the police. So a complaint should be addressed to the local chief officer rather than the Police Complaints Authority; in the case of senior officers (above Chief Superintendent) outside London, it will be referred on to the local police authority. If the complaint is not against a senior officer, the chief officer then has to decide whether the complaint is 'suitable for informal resolution'. This will only be possible if the person who has made the complaint agrees, and the chief officer is satisfied that the conduct complained of, if proved, would not justify a criminal or disciplinary charge. Informal resolution of complaints is not explained in the Act but the Home Office leaflet makes it clear that it may result in an explanation or an apology to the complainant, in appropriate cases.

If a complaint is not suitable for informal resolution, or if informal resolution fails, then the complaint must be investigated by another police officer. But this does not apply to complaints against senior officers which would not, even if proved, justify a criminal or disciplinary charge.

In addition, certain types of complaint must be referred to the Police Complaints Authority. These include complaints alleging that the conduct complained of resulted in death or serious injury, and allegations of actual bodily harm, bribery, or a serious arrestable offence. The chief officer has a discretionary power to refer any other complaint to the Authority. Serious matters can be referred on even if there has not yet been a complaint. And the Authority itself, which is allowed to receive complaints direct from members of the public, can require the police to submit details of any complaint to it.

The Police Complaints Authority must supervise the investigation of a complaint alleging death or serious injury, and it may supervise the investigation of any other complaint if it thinks this is desirable in the public interest. The complaint will be investigated by a police officer, but the Authority can effectively decide who that officer will be. The Authority has an important power to tell the police how the investigation should be conducted. At the end of the investigation the investigating officer submits a report to the Authority which then has to say whether it was satisfied with the way the investigation was conducted. Until then no disciplinary proceedings, or – unless there are exceptional circumstances – criminal proceedings, can be brought in respect of the complaint.

Whether or not the investigation of a complaint has been supervised by the Police Complaints Authority, the investigating officer has to submit a report on it. If it relates to a senior officer it must be sent to the Director of Public Prosecutions unless it's clear no offence has been committed. If it relates to a junior officer, the chief officer has to decide whether the report indicates that an offence may have been committed by one of his officers and if so whether the officer ought to be charged with it. If he decides the answer to both those questions is 'yes', he must send a copy of the report to the Director of Public Prosecutions. If the chief officer decides that an offence may have been committed but the officer should not be charged – or if he decides that none of his officers has committed a criminal offence – he must tell the Police Complaints Authority whether he is bringing disciplinary charges instead (and if not, why not). If the accused officer has admitted the disciplinary charges, the Authority need not be told until the disciplinary proceedings are over.

The Act makes it clear that the Police Complaints Authority must be sent reports on all cases involving junior officers where a complaint which has been investigated has not led to criminal proceedings, regardless of whether the Authority supervised the investigation. The Authority then can have the papers sent to the Director of Public Prosecutions if it thinks an officer should be charged with a crime. It also has the power to make the chief officer bring disciplinary proceedings, and in such cases two members of the Authority sit with the chief officers to hear the charge.

Section 101 of the Act makes racially discriminatory behaviour by the police a specific disciplinary offence.

Section 104 says that where a policeman has been convicted or acquitted of a criminal offence he can't then be charged with substantially the same offence against discipline – although he can, if convicted, be charged with the disciplinary offence of 'criminal conduct'.

The Home Office leaflet *Complaints against the Police* points out that whatever the result of your complaint you still have the right to sue the police if you feel you should be paid compensation for something they've done – for example, if a police officer has damaged your property. But it adds that in such cases the official complaint investigation may be held up until the civil action has been completed. It also points out that police officers can sue people who deliberately make false complaints against them.

## Public order

The law of public order is in the process of change. A Public Order Bill will no doubt keep MPs and peers busy for much of 1986, and by 1987 it's likely there'll be a new Act in force. We can't give you a detailed summary of the new law because the bill hadn't been published at the time we wrote this book, and in any case it may be amended as it goes through Parliament. But what we can do is to summarise the government's plans to reform public order law, outlined in their White Paper of May 1985. People sometimes assume that after a White Paper is published the government then sets to work drafting a bill to put the proposals into effect; in fact, the bill is usually settled first and only then can a White Paper be written to explain (and, if necessary, justify) the government's intentions. So the chances are that when we come to write a new edition of this book – after the Act is in force – we won't have to make many changes to the sections that follow.

## Marches and processions

Under the White Paper proposals, anyone organising a march will in future have to give the police seven days notice of their intentions. There will be an exception for processions of a religious, educational or ceremonial character customarily held in an area. And there will be another exception to allow marches to be held with shorter notice so long as the organisers tell the police 'as soon as reasonably practicable': this is to allow immediate protests over some urgent local event, such as a child being injured at a dangerous road junction. If an organiser of a march or procession fails to give advance notice he or she can be prosecuted under the proposed new law and fined up to £400; the marchers would not, however, be committing an offence.

The Public Order Act 1936 gives the police power to ban marches outright if they expect 'serious public disorder'. This will remain unchanged. But these banning orders have sometimes gone further than was necessary: a blanket ban on marches stops the good guys as well as the baddies. The White Paper said that in future the police would have the power to ban a single march or procession instead – a refinement which was welcomed by the National Council for Civil Liberties and the Legal Action Group. But in November 1985 the new Home Secretary, Mr Douglas Hurd, said this provision had been dropped from the forthcoming bill after representations from the police. Under the government's proposals, anyone organising a banned march can be fined £1000 or given three months in prison. In future the police will be able to arrest anyone taking part in a banned march; the maximum fine will be £400.

At present, instead of banning them, the police can impose conditions on marches if they expect 'serious public disorder'. These conditions include prescribing the route to be taken by the procession. The new Act will make it clear that serious public disorder can include serious damage to property. But it will also widen the powers of the police to impose these conditions by adding two new cases where the conditions can be imposed. The first is where they believe the march will cause 'serious disruption to the normal life of the community'. The White Paper suggests this new power could be used to stop demonstrators marching down Oxford Street during shopping hours. The National Council for Civil Liberties says it could be used to stop a large march which would take a long time to complete. The second new case where the police will be able to impose conditions is to prevent 'the coercion of individuals'. The example given is of a National Front march which had been designed to stop another march by the Troops Out Movement: 'stop this vermin . . . don't let them march'. The government White Paper says that demonstrators will be able to challenge police conditions by applying to the Divisional Court for judicial review. But we doubt how effective this remedy will be: as we explained earlier, judicial review deals only with the way a decision is taken, not with the merits of the decision. The Divisional Court is not a court of appeal from the body under review and will not substitute its judgment or discretion for that of the body under review. However, in a radio interview about his White Paper broadcast on the day it was published the then Home Secretary, Mr Leon Brittan, dismissed this argument. His successor, Mr Douglas Hurd, said judicial review was a sensible precaution against any abuse of power by the police: a High Court judge would have to decide whether the police had acted reasonably.

Marchers who disobey police conditions, and people who organise a prohibited procession, can at present be found guilty of an offence under the Public Order Act 1936. In future, the police will have a specific power to arrest them. Anyone who organises a march contrary to police directions, or who incites others to disobey the conditions, will in future be liable to three months in prison or a fine of £1000. Marchers who disobey police conditions will be liable to a maximum fine of £400.

## Demonstrations and meetings

The White Paper's proposals on how to deal with what it calls 'static demonstrations and meetings' involve important changes in the law. Up to now they've not been covered by the Public

Order Act, which only applies to marches and processions. Under the new plans, demonstrations and meetings will now be covered by some of the new restrictions.

There's no power at present to ban demonstrations outright, and the government doesn't intend to introduce one in the future. There's no need to give the police notice of a demonstration – and this won't change either. These decisions are apparently acceptable to the police, and also to the National Council for Civil Liberties. So far, so good. But read on.

The government intends to bring static demonstrations in the open air (but not those in closed premises) within the new restrictions for marches we've just mentioned. This means the police will be able to impose restrictions on demonstrations if they reasonably expect public disorder (which includes serious damage to property); or serious disruption to the life of the community (which could result from a demonstration in a busy shopping street or outside an embassy); or the coercion of individuals (which the White Paper says happened to men going to work during the miners strike of 1984/85).

What conditions can they impose? They won't be able to stop a demonstration going ahead at the time fixed by the organisers, but there will be three important restrictions open to the police. If they expect one of the problems mentioned in the previous paragraph, they'll be able to impose conditions on the size, location, and duration of the meeting.

The National Council for Civil Liberties says these conditions would 'virtually amount to the very ban that the White Paper rightly says is unacceptable'. The NCCL's legal officer, Marie Staunton, offered an example. 'If the police were to instruct the organisers of an all-night vigil outside the Home Office to stand half a mile away, restrict their members to two and stay for only fifteen minutes, the effect would be virtually the same as a complete ban,' she said. Anticipating this argument, the Home Office says judicial review will be available to challenge such a decision, just as it will be with marches. But the objections we mentioned earlier still apply.

What happens if you disregard the police conditions? Read

the White Paper carefully, and you'll see that anyone taking part in a demonstration who knowingly disobeys police instructions will be committing an offence for which the maximum penalty is a fine of £400. The organisers of such a demonstration could get up to three months in prison and/or a fine of £1000. There will be a power to arrest offenders.

It's worth pausing for a moment to take in what this means. Open air static demonstrations include meetings, counter-demonstrations outside meetings, demonstrations outside embassies, lobbies of Parliament, pickets, demonstrations in support of pickets, political rallies, religious meetings, pop festivals, and football matches. So in future the police are to have power to arrest pickets who disobey police instructions. If the powers had been in force in the summer of 1985 they would no doubt have been used to deal with two groups of people who caught the people's attention – the 'hippies' who tried to camp at Stonehenge, and football hooligans.

The Labour party's immediate reaction to these proposals was given by Mr Gerald Kaufman. 'The Government is intending to create a criminal law on picketing,' he told MPs. 'It will place the police in an intolerable position of taking political decisions on such occasions. It will erode their independence and turn them into the reluctant agents of this government's policies.' Mr Brittan's view, however, was that 'freedom of association and freedom of speech are essential to any democratic society. They must be given full and effective protection. But,' the then Home Secretary added, 'people also have the right to protection against being bullied, hurt, intimidated or obstructed, whatever the motive of those responsible may be, whether they are violent demonstrators, rioters, intimidatory mass pickets or soccer hooligans.'

## Common Law Public Order offences in general

Many public order offences are currently part of the common law, which means they've been built up by the judges over the centuries. The government intends to codify most of them by replacing the common law with what is expected to become the Public

Order Act 1986. But in codifying the law Parliament has the opportunity to change the law – hence the political arguments over what the new Act should say.

The White Paper on public order law has an excellent summary of the law on the breach of the peace, itself derived from Brownlie's *Law of Public Order* edited by Michael Supperstone. It says: 'the concept of a breach of the peace derives from the early days of the common law. Breach of the peace is not in England and Wales a criminal offence, although it is in Scotland; but it forms the basis of important police powers. If the police reasonably apprehend an imminent breach of the peace they may take any action which is necessary to control or prevent it, including arresting those who are responsible. The police may limit numbers in the particular place in order to prevent breaches of the peace: it was under this common law power that the police stopped and turned back pickets during the miners' dispute, and turned back National Front members outside Wakefield in January 1984 after they had been banned from marching in neighbouring towns. The common law power to disperse an unlawful assembly derives from the police's general power to control breaches of the peace. The police may also bring anyone who threatens the peace before the courts to enter into a recognizance and find sureties to keep the peace or to be of good behaviour, or in default to be imprisoned for up to six months. This preventive power to bind someone over to be of good behaviour is traced back to the Justices of the Peace Act 1361, and is still frequently used in public order cases.'

The White Paper then goes on to the offences of riot, rout, unlawful assembly and affray which were extensions of the concept of breach of the peace established in the sixteenth century. They all involve the idea of open force or public violence which causes terror to other people.

## Riot

Riot at common law was committed when three or more people in execution of a common purpose used force or violence so as to alarm people of reasonable firmness, and with intent to help one another by force if necessary against anyone who may have opposed them.

Charges of riot (and other public order offences) were brought against miners involved in the strike of 1984/85. The charges rebounded on the prosecution – of nearly a hundred miners arrested after violent scenes outside the Orgreave coking plant in May 1984, the prosecution failed to win a single conviction for riot or unlawful assembly. In August 1985 the prosecution dropped riot charges against 39 of the men who were due to stand trial; uppermost in the prosecution's mind was the fact that a month earlier they'd decided to abandon the trial on the 48th day of 14 other men charged with rioting at Orgreave.

In another case 18 miners were charged with riot and affray following disturbances at the end of a union rally in Nottinghamshire. All pleaded not guilty, and all were acquitted after (or, in some cases, during) a trial lasting three months. Charges against other men were then dropped.

The White Paper, agreeing with a proposal from the Law Commission, proposed a new statutory offence of riot: where twelve or more persons are present together, whether in a public or private place, using or threatening unlawful violence to persons or property for some common purpose (which may be inferred from their conduct) and their conduct, taken together, is such as would cause a person of reasonable firmness present at the scene to fear for his personal safety, each of them who uses unlawful violence for the common purpose commits the offence of riot. The offence would require the consent of the Director of Public Prosecutions to the institution of proceedings and would be triable on indictment with a maximum penalty of life imprisonment and a fine.

This increases the minimum number required for riot from three to twelve, and introduces the requirement that each defendant must be shown to have personally used unlawful violence – either to people or to property.

## Violent disorder

At present there's a common law offence of unlawful assembly, the essence of which (according to Professor Brownlie) is an actual disturbance or present tendency to create a reasonable apprehension of a breach of the peace. The White Paper says this charge may be brought when a demonstration results in violence, or when one group deliberately sets out to attack another. We've already seen how the prosecution failed to win convictions for unlawful assembly after the disturbances at Orgreave: 40 charges were dropped at one hearing in August 1985.

A new offence of 'violent disorder' will replace unlawful assembly; the White Paper says it will also be used in some cases where charges of riot would be brought under the common law. The government intends that it will be the normal charge for serious outbreaks of public disorder, but it will cover a wide range of possible disturbances: where three or more persons are present together using or threatening unlawful violence to persons or property, whether in a public or private place, and their conduct, taken together, is such as would cause a person of reasonable firmness if present at the scene to fear for his personal safety, each of those persons who uses or threatens unlawful violence commits the offence of violent disorder. The offence would be triable either by a magistrates' court or before a jury with a maximum penalty in the Crown Court of five years imprisonment and a fine.

The words 'or threatens' were not included in the Law Commission's proposed definition. They proposed a different offence of 'conduct intended or likely to cause fear or provoke violence', but the government says running this and Section 5 of the Public Order Act 1936 together and widening violent disorder will enable all the members of a group to be tried together even though some may only have threatened violence. The Legal Action Group has criticised this change for building a serious offence on a vague concept.

Violent disorder differs from riot by not requiring a 'common purpose'; by requiring only three people; and by dealing with people who only threaten violence.

## Affray

The present common law offence of affray consists of unlawful fighting, or a display of force without actual violence, in such a way that a person of reasonably firm character might expect to be terrified.

The government has accepted the Law Commission's proposed new statutory offence: where one or more people use or threaten unlawful violence against another, whether in a public or private place, and the conduct of those using or threatening unlawful violence is such as would cause a person of reasonable firmness if present at the scene to fear for his personal safety, each of them commits the offence of affray. The offence would again be triable by magistrates or in the Crown Court where the maximum penalty would be three years imprisonment and a fine.

There is little change here from the common law. Affray is the most widely used of the common law public order offences. It's used to charge people who take part in spontaneous fights at pubs and dance halls.

## Rout

A rout is an unlawful assembly which hasn't quite developed into a riot. The offence is obsolete and is being abolished.

## Threatening words or behaviour

Section 5 of the Public Order Act 1936 (as amended) says that:

> Any person who in any public place or any public meeting
>
> (a)   uses threatening, abusive or insulting words or behaviour, or
>
> (b)   distributes or displays any writing, sign or visible representation which is threatening, abusive or insulting,

with intent to provoke a breach of the peace or whereby a breach of the peace is likely to be occasioned, shall be guilty of an offence and shall on summary conviction be liable to imprisonment for a term not exceeding six months or to a fine not exceeding £2,000 or to both.

This is to be redrafted to take account of the Law Commission's proposals on conduct intended or likely to cause fear or provoke violence. It will now read (with the changes in italics):

Any person who, whether in a public *or private place*, uses threatening, abusive or insulting words or behaviour which is intended or likely

(a) *to cause another person to fear unlawful violence, or*

(b) *to provoke the use of unlawful violence by another*

shall be guilty of an offence, and shall on summary conviction be liable to imprisonment for a term not exceeding six months or to a fine not exceeding the statutory maximum or both. (The statutory maximum in the magistrates' court is at present £2,000.)

## Disorderly conduct

One of the most controversial proposals in this part of the White Paper is that there should be a new offence penalising 'disorderly conduct'. Examples are given of minor acts of hooliganism which the government thinks it might not be appropriate to prosecute under the newly-amended section 5 of the 1936 Act: hooligans on housing estates causing disturbances in the common parts of blocks of flats, blockading entrances, throwing things down the stairs, banging on doors, peering in at windows, and knocking over dustbins; groups of youths persistently shouting abuse and obscenities or pestering people waiting to catch public transport or to enter a hall or cinema: someone turning out the lights in a crowded dance hall, in a way likely to cause panic; and rowdy behaviour in the streets late at night which alarms local residents.

To deal with this sort of thing the White Paper proposed and the government later decided that there should be a new offence to cover threatening, abusive, insulting or disorderly words or behaviour in, or within view of, a public place which causes substantial alarm, harassment or distress. The White Paper stressed that the behaviour must actually cause alarm, and the alarm must be substantial. Nevertheless, this is one of the few proposals on which the White Paper invited comment, which may have reflected misgivings on the part of ministers and their officials. In favour of the new offence is the Association of Chief Police Officers. The Association has not published its response to the White Paper, but the author of that response, the Chief Constable of Essex Mr Robert Bunyard, told his Association's conference that 'people whose lives are made miserable by hooligans have a right to such a law'. Too often, officers dealing with such incidents had to pretend they had powers which they didn't possess. 'There is more danger', said Mr Bunyard, 'in leaving them without a legitimate power than in possible abuse of that power.'

However, the proposals are opposed by the National Council for Civil Liberties, and also the Legal Action Group, which says the proposed offence of disorderly conduct is undesirable in principle, unworkably vague, and unnecessary. Conduct that cannot be brought under section 5 of the Public Order Act 1936 (because it is not likely to cause a breach of the peace) cannot be defined in a manner sufficiently precise to found a criminal offence, according to LAG. While the behaviour outlined in the White Paper – peering in at windows, knocking over dustbins, rowdy behaviour in the streets late at night alarming local residents – may be socially undesirable, LAG says it is not conduct which should be criminalised. In the view of the Legal Action Group, 'it should not be left to the police to determine what is socially unacceptable behaviour. The existing criminal law provides adequate remedies for behaviour causing damage or constituting assault; the proposal would create a "sus" offence which Parliament has already rejected.'

Questioned about this on *Law in Action* in November 1985, the Home Secretary, Douglas Hurd, said that Parliament would want to see how carefully the offence of disorderly conduct had been drafted when the bill was published. 'But when you see the actual definition,' he said, 'I think you'll find it's a long way from "sus".' Mr Hurd said the government were not trying to penalise high spirits. There would have to be a victim – someone who was distressed, alarmed or harassed.

By the time the bill finally appeared, the government had dropped the requirement that the alarm, harassment or distress should be 'substantial'. What's more, there's no longer any need for the behaviour actually to alarm, harass or distress anyone; the defendant can be convicted if there is reason for him to believe this was merely 'likely'. The police can arrest people for this offence if they ignore a warning to stop. The maximum fine is to be £400.

## TERRORISM

The Prevention of Terrorism (Temporary Provisions) Act 1984 is the latest in a series of 'temporary' Acts, the first of which was introduced after the Birmingham pub bombing of 1974.

Part I, which does not apply in Northern Ireland, makes it an offence to belong to the Irish Republican Army or the Irish National Liberation Army. It's also an offence to raise money for them. Other organisations concerned in terrorism which occurs in England, Wales or Scotland, and which is connected with Northern Irish affairs, may also be proscribed by the Home Secretary in the same way. 'Terrorism' is defined as the use of violence for political ends, and includes any use of violence for the purpose of putting people in fear.

Part II of the Act restricts freedom of movement within the United Kingdom. It allows the Home Secretary to exclude from England, Wales and Scotland anyone concerned in terrorism or who may enter Great Britain with a view to being concerned in terrorism. There are similar powers to exclude people from

Northern Ireland, or the United Kingdom as a whole. The acts of terrorism to which this part of the Act applies are acts of terrorism designed to influence public opinion or government policy with respect to affairs in Northern Ireland. There are various safeguards, and a person who is excluded has the right in certain circumstances to a personal interview with an adviser nominated by the Home Secretary. The Home Secretary must reconsider his decision to make such an 'exclusion order' in the light of the adviser's report.

Part III of the Act makes it an offence punishable with up to five years imprisonment for a person who has information which he believes might help prevent an act of terrorism connected with Northern Irish affairs, or lead to the arrest of a terrorist, not to disclose that information as soon as practicable to the police (or, in Northern Ireland, the army).

Part IV of the Act allows the police to arrest people and detain them for up to 48 hours. The Home Secretary may extend this period for up to five days, making a week in all. The people liable to arrest are those reasonably suspected of being members of the proscribed organisations (the IRA and INLA); people subject to an exclusion order; or those concerned in terrorism. Terrorism here is not restricted to Northern Ireland, but it does not cover acts connected solely with the affairs of England, Wales and Scotland. The Act also sets up a system of port controls on people entering or leaving Great Britain or Northern Ireland who may be searched and examined to see whether they are concerned with terrorism or subject to an exclusion order. Regulations made under the Act make it an offence to withhold information from an officer carrying out such an examination. As Fiona Hargreaves and Howard Levenson point out, this is an exception to the general right of silence and avoidance of self-incrimination. A person being examined can be detained for 48 hours, and this again may be extended to a total of seven days by the Home Secretary.

# SECRETS

We wrote earlier of how juries who refuse to convict in the face of the evidence can sometimes bring about the repeal of a discredited law (page 78). Few laws are as discredited as the Official Secrets Act 1911, but although governments may now be reluctant to use part of the statute except in clear-cut cases, the present government has no plans to amend or repeal it. The Act passed through all its parliamentary stages in the House of Commons in 40 minutes, although it had been debated in the Lords some weeks earlier. Perhaps not surprisingly, the important section 2 was never mentioned during the parliamentary debates.

## Section 1 of the Official Secrets Act 1911

Section 1 of the Act prescribes what are described in the marginal note as 'penalties for spying'. But the wording goes much further, and in 1978 the section was used – unsuccessfully – against two journalists, Crispin Aubrey and Duncan Campbell, who were charged with the former soldier John Berry in the famous ABC case.

Section 1 as amended makes it an offence if any person, for any purpose prejudicial to the safety or interests of the State, approaches a prohibited place; makes a sketch or note which might be useful to an enemy; or obtains or communicates any information which might be useful to an enemy. The maximum sentence is 14 years in prison, but longer sentences have been passed on spies by making sentences on separate counts run consecutively.

## Section 2 of the Offical Secrets Act 1911

The main offence created by section 2 is the unauthorised communication of official information by anyone who holds or has held office under the Crown. But again the wording goes much further, and by frequent and clumsy use of the word 'or' manages to create over two thousand differently worded offences. It covers

110

information which has no relation to the security of the State. The information need not be confidential. It extends to government contractors and their staff. And the section also makes it an offence to receive such information, unless the person who receives it can prove this was against his wishes. Anybody – not just a civil servant – who receives information which has been made or obtained in contravention of the Act is not allowed to disclose it without authorisation. The maximum penalty is two years imprisonment and a fine.

Section 2 has of course been endlessly criticised. Perhaps one of the best argued cases was put in 1971 by Sir Peter Rawlinson as he then was, the Attorney General in the Conservative government of 1970–74. These were Lord Rawlinson's official submissions to Lord Franks' enquiry into the Act:

> In my opinion section 2 is in unnecessarily wide terms, because it embraces all types of official information regardless of its importance or of the damage which could result from disclosure. Much information in the hands of Civil Servants and others can be disclosed without any damage to the interest of the State, and it is wrong in principle that a criminal statute should make it an offence to do something which is not contrary to the public interest. I would welcome therefore a solution which narrowed the categories of information to which the section applies.
>
> At the same time, the effect of the section is not necessarily so wide as is sometimes stated. It only applies to the unauthorised communication of information. Unlike some other statutes, section 2 does not in itself prevent those in authority from allowing official information to be published, by giving express or implied authorisation for this to be done. The width of the section thus depends to a large extent on the application of Government policy concerning disclosure of information rather than on any legal formula.

It is of course the Attorney General who has to decide whether a prosecution should go ahead (under either section 1 or section 2). According to Lord Rawlinson, the Attorney of the day takes four factors into account: the strength of the evidence; the degree of culpability of the potential defendant; the damage to the public interest which has resulted from disclosure; and the effect of prosecution on the public interest.

And these criteria were endorsed by the present Attorney General, Sir Michael Havers, in a speech he made in June 1985. Sir Michael said that he too thought section 2 was too widely drawn. He recalled that the government had tried to amend it in 1979 without success. Sir Michael went on:

> Given that this is the situation, the more immediate question for me is how I operate section 2 as it stands. Do I simply sit back and say I won't prosecute anyone? If I took such a view I would be, quite rightly, accused of a serious derogation of my duty as Attorney General, for I do have a duty to enforce the criminal law. I have no right, nor must I seek to usurp the functions of Parliament by effectively repealing legislation myself. Parliament has given me a discretion as to which prosecutions I should bring but not a discretion to say for all time I will not bring any proceedings under this section. As I have a discretion, should I then say to myself – well I will only bring proceedings where there are serious security implications, or only in line with the recommendations in the Franks Report? Likewise I believe it would be a remarkable constitutional innovation for me to proceed automatically as if the law had been amended by the Franks Report. While section 2 stands I and my successors have to recognise that Parliament has given us a discretion and it would be wrong for us to fetter that discretion in any way. So how do I exercise my discretion? Every case has to be judged on its own facts and merits, and I make no apology for saying that I shall continue to operate section 2 in the same way as any other criminal offence. Firstly I have to decide whether the evidence is sufficient to afford a reasonable prospect of a conviction. Secondly, assuming that that is the case, I then go

on to decide whether the public interest requires the institution of criminal proceedings. I see myself as the guardian against unreasonable and oppressive prosecutions and that in my view is the proper and traditional role of the Attorney General when deciding whether or not proceedings should be instituted.

In defence of section 2 I should emphasise that not every decision to prosecute under it is controversial. Many cases are prosecuted in the magistrates court where no one, I venture to suggest, would doubt that the proceedings should have been brought. During my stewardship of section 2 I have authorised several sets of proceedings where a policeman or a police employee has passed confidential information, usually for monetary gain, from the police national computer to which he has had access through his position. However, even though in these cases the decision to prosecute is not controversial, I accept that in other cases my decision can be very controversial indeed.

In the forefront of Sir Michael Havers' mind was his decision to prosecute Clive Ponting for wrongful communication of information under section 2. It is not an offence under the Act for somebody to pass such information to 'a person to whom it is in the interest of the State his duty to communicate it'. Clive Ponting's defence – apparently tried for the first time – was that it was in the interest of the State to pass documents to Tam Dalyell MP about the sinking of the Argentine cruiser *General Belgrano* during the Falklands war. Mr Justice McCowan rejected this construction of the statute. He agreed with the prosecution view that 'interest of the State' meant 'the policies laid down for it by the recognised organs of government and authority'. 'The policies of the State were the policies of the government then in power', the judge told the jury; 'it cannot be in the interests of the State to have leaked these documents to Dalyell'.

This view of the law, which was in effect rejected by the jury, was subsequently also criticised by academic writers, such as

113

Professor Graham Zellick. He suggested the Attorney General should have used his powers to refer the case to the Court of Appeal for an authoritative view of the law. The Attorney's Legal Secretary, the senior official in his department, replied that Sir Michael had not referred the case 'because he regarded Mr Justice McCowan's ruling on the law as correct and fully in accordance with authority'.

### 'Signing' the Official Secrets Act

All civil servants are required to 'sign' the Official Secrets Act when they're first appointed; for many years BBC journalists had to do so too. Clive Ponting, in his book *The Right to Know*, reproduces the form civil servants have to sign. To reprint it is of course a breach of the Official Secrets Act. Here it is:

> Declaration. To be signed by members of Government Departments on appointment and, where desirable, by non-civil servants on first being given access to Government information.
>
> My attention has been drawn to the provisions of the Official Secrets Act set out on the back of this document and I am fully aware of the serious consequences which may follow any breach of those provisions. . . . I am aware that I should not divulge any information gained by me as a result of my appointment to any unauthorised person, either orally or in writing, without the previous official sanction in writing of the department appointing me, to which written application should be made and two copies of the proposed publication be forwarded.

It's surprising how many people think that by signing this form they become subject to the Official Secrets Act. The Act makes no mention of any form. There's no suggestion in the Act that the legislation only applies to people who know about it. Both section 1 and section 2 begin with the words 'If any person . . .'. Ignorance of the law is no defence, and it would be a pretty feeble piece of legislation if a spy could escape 42 years in prison by saying he was only familiar with statutes passed since, say, the First World War. Nor can there be any justification for punishing a breach of the Act more heavily because there was proof a civil servant had been told about the Act's provisions. So if you are asked to sign a meaningless piece of paper when you start a new job, and you fancy a quiet life, why not sign?

## CROWN PROSECUTION SERVICE

A major change in the criminal justice system of England and Wales takes effect in 1986. From April in the ill-fated metropolitan counties, and from October 1986 in London and the rest of England and Wales, a new Crown Prosecution Service is responsible for the conduct of all proceedings instituted by the police. The creation of an independent prosecution service was recommended by the Royal Commission on Criminal Procedure in 1981; it said there were a number of defects in the system which then existed. Too many cases were reaching the courts only to be dismissed because of insufficient evidence, it said, and there were wide variations across the country in deciding whether to go ahead with a prosecution. The government agreed, but decided the new system should be nationally accountable, rather than accountable to local police authorities as the Royal Commission had proposed. In many ways the new English Crown Prosecutor has a role similar to that of the procurator fiscal who has handled prosecutions in Scotland for more than a century.

The head of the Crown Prosecution Service is the Director of Public Prosecutions, Sir Thomas Hetherington. Under the Prosecution of Offences Act 1985, he and his staff are given the duty of taking over the conduct of all criminal proceedings instituted by the police, except for certain minor offences where the defendant pleads guilty by post. The Crown Prosecution Service reviews cases before court hearings to see whether there is sufficient evidence and whether prosecution is in the public interest. The new service is responsible for providing advocates to present cases

115

in Magistrates' Courts, and briefs counsel to appear on its behalf in the Crown Court. So the police continue to investigate crime and bring charges, but under the new system the Crown Prosecution Service decides whether they should go ahead.

The Director of Public Prosecutions is appointed by the Attorney General, who is responsible for the 'superintendence' of his work. In practice the two men are in almost daily contact.

The Attorney General made it clear in a White Paper at the end of 1984 that the great majority of prosecuting decisions would be taken in the Crown Prosecution Service's local offices rather than in London by the Director of Public Prosecutions. Indeed some cases which had to go to the Director under the old system are dealt with locally under the new arrangements: these include murders where the evidence is not in dispute and the defence is one of provocation, self-defence, or diminished responsibility. Attempted murder is still referred to the Director of Public Prosecutions because of the problems in proving intent; he also sees cases involving major frauds, obscene publications, and allegations against the police.

## Prosecution guidelines

How then does the Director decide whether to go ahead with a prosecution? It's well known that in general he's guided by the 'fifty-one per cent rule' – in other words a prosecution should only go ahead if the chances of a conviction are better than fifty-fifty. This is explained more fully in a little-known memorandum issued by the Attorney General which will no doubt form the basis of Crown Prosecutors' decisions.

The first question to be answered by a prosecutor, according to the memorandum, is whether there's enough evidence to make conviction more likely than acquittal. But an even higher standard is set if an acquittal could be unfortunate – for example an unsuccessful prosecution of an allegedly obscene book could increase sales.

The next question is whether a prosecution is in the public interest. On this point the Director and the Attorney refer back to remarks made to MPs one evening early in 1951 by the then Labour Attorney General, Sir Hartley Shawcross: 'It has never been the rule in this country – I hope it never will be – that suspected criminal offences must automatically be the subject of prosecution. Indeed the very first regulations under which the Director of Public Prosecutions worked provided that he should ... prosecute "wherever it appears that the offence or the circumstances of its commission is or are of such a character that a prosecution in respect thereof is required in the public interest". That is still the dominant consideration.'

Lord Shawcross continued by saying that regard must be had to 'the effect which the prosecution, successful or unsuccessful as the case may be, would have upon public morale and order, and with any other considerations affecting public policy'.

So what factors are taken into account by the Director of Public Prosecutions?

*Likely penalty*: When the circumstances of an offence, especially if triable on indictment, are not particularly serious, and the probable penalty on conviction would only be a conditional or absolute discharge, he believes it would not normally be in the public interest to prosecute.

*Staleness*: The Director is slow to prosecute if the last offence was committed three or more years before the probable date of trial, unless, despite its staleness, an immediate custodial sentence of the same length is likely to be imposed. Less regard is paid to staleness, however, if it has been contributed to by the proposed defendant himself, or the complexity of the case has necessitated lengthy police investigation.

*Youth*: The stigma of a conviction can cause irreparable harm to the future prospects of a young person, and careful consideration is given to the possibility of dealing with him or her by means of a caution. Regard is had to previous character, parental attitude and likelihood of the offence being repeated.

*Old age and infirmity*: The older or more infirm the offender, the more reluctant the Director of Public Prosecutions is to prosecute

117

unless there is a real possibility of repetition or the offence is of such gravity that it is impossible to overlook. He also has to consider whether the accused is likely to be fit enough to stand trial.

*Mental illness or stress*: The defence solicitor, knowing that the police are investigating his client's conduct, may sometimes send to the Director of Public Prosecutions a psychiatric report to the effect that the accused is suffering from some form of mental illness and that the strain of criminal proceedings will lead to a considerable and permanent worsening of his condition. This is nearly as worrying as, say, a report that the accused has a weak heart and that the shock of prosecution may be fatal.

The Director of Public Prosecutions will normally try to arrange for an independent examination and will in any event give anxious consideration to such reports as he may receive. This is a difficult field because in some instances the accused may have become mentally disturbed or depressed by the mere fact that his misconduct has been discovered and the Director is sometimes dubious about a prognosis that criminal proceedings will adversely affect his condition to a significant extent.

*Sexual offences*: Where the girl or youth has been a willing party to the offence the Director of Public Prosecutions takes into account her or his age, the relative age of the parties and whether or not there was any element of seduction or corruption.

If the Director of Public Prosecutions still couldn't make up his mind, he would throw into the scales the good or bad character of the accused, the atitude of the local community and any information about the prevalence of the particular offence in the area or nationally. Should doubt still remain, the Director believes that the scales should normally be tipped in favour of prosecution because, if the balance is so even, his view is that the final arbiter must be the court.

# Prisons

The then Home Secretary, Mr Leon Brittan, said in August 1985 that the prison service was 'hard pressed'. His critics have spoken of 'prisons in crisis', and the only people who disagree with that description are those who say it's impossible for a crisis to continue as long as this one has.

Between September 1984 and August 1985 the prison population rose from 42,200 to a peak of 48,200. The Home Secretary said this was because a larger number of defendants were being dealt with by the Crown Court, and a larger proportion of them were given a custodial sentence. The average length of certain types of sentence was also increasing.

The Home Secretary's response was to create 2,000 new prison places in 1985 by reorganising existing accommodation and building a new prison, which might eventually take 1,000 prisoners, at a wartime RAF station near Doncaster, and is expected to hold 750 prisoners by the spring of 1986. His long-term plans included encouraging the Probation Service to provide non-custodial alternatives, trying to reduce the number of prisoners held on remand, and trying to keep minor offenders, such as drunks, out of the criminal justice system altogether. But as Mr Brittan acknowledged, these measures were not going to solve the problems of the prison system overnight.

NACRO, the highly-respected National Association for the Care and Resettlement of Offenders, calculated – in November 1985 – that the United Kingdom imprisons more people, both in absolute numbers and relative to its population, than any other major Western European nation except Turkey. In 1983 the United Kingdom locked up proportionately twice as many people as France and nearly four times as many as Greece. NACRO calculated that fewer than one in five of people convicted in England and Wales had committed crimes involving violence, sex or robbery. Six men out of ten leaving prison establishments and four women in every ten were back before the courts within two years.

It was on these figures that NACRO drew its conclusions.

'Advocates of harsher penal policies have promoted the myth that sentencing has become increasingly lenient and that a tougher approach would help to reduce crime,' it said. 'In fact, this country uses prison on a far greater scale than our European neighbours and has sharply increased its use of custody over the last decade, Moreover,' NACRO said, 'imprisonment has proved markedly unsuccessful in reducing offending.'

It is in this context that we must look at prisoners' rights. Overcrowding means that in many cases prisoners are held two or three to a cell built for one person in Victorian times. Prison workshops and educational centres were having to close because of lack of staff.

Prisoners' 'rights', such as visits, letters, association, home leave, parole and so on, are in fact privileges – which can be withdrawn for bad behaviour. The Prison Rules lay down the conditions under which prisoners are confined, and breaches are judged by the Governor, who has the power to caution, remove or delay privileges, exclude from associated work, stop earnings, confine a prisoner to his cell, or stop remission. For more serious offences a Board of Visitors adjudicates.

Boards of Visitors – in the great British tradition of giving important responsibilities to well-meaning amateurs – are independent voluntary bodies of lay men and women appointed by the Home Secretary to monitor conditions in individual prison establishments. They must not be confused with prison visitors, who are also volunteers appointed by the Home Office but with the task of visiting selected prisoners to keep them in touch with the community.

Boards of Visitors have little executive control within prisons, but they're given virtually unlimited rights of access, wide-ranging powers to punish prisoners charged with disciplinary offences, and the ability to make their own views known directly to the Home Secretary.

As we've said, Boards of Visitors adjudicate on prisoners charged with serious offences against prison discipline – five per cent of the total. The largest categories punished are escape from legal custody, and assaults; with loss of remission being by far the most frequently awarded punishment. However, in October 1985 the Home Secretary, Mr Hurd, announced that there were to be new arrangements to deal with prisoners charged with serious offences against prison discipline. In a cautious written answer he said he accepted the fundamental conclusion of a report on prison discipline which he'd just received. The report – from a committee chaired by the industrialist Mr Peter Prior – said the disciplinary role of prison Boards of Visitors should be transferred to new tribunals chaired by lawyers. It was because Boards of Visitors combined their disciplinary powers with their 'pastoral' or 'watchdog' roles that the Prior report said many prisoners saw them as part of prison management rather than as independent arbitrators. Hence the proposed new system of independent Prison Disciplinary Tribunals which Prior said should be set up to hear serious cases. The maximum penalty which the new tribunal could impose for one offence would be four months' loss of remission. The tribunal would be able to decide whether a prisoner should be legally represented.

The Prior Committee also proposed that some very serious offences which are at present dealt with as part of the prison disciplinary system should become criminal offences. The courts would then be able to impose an additional six months' imprisonment on a prisoner who assaulted a prison officer in the execution of his duty, and up to ten years for mutiny in a prison.

There will have to be legislation if these plans are to be put into effect; the earliest a bill could become law would be the summer of 1987. The Prior proposals were welcomed by NACRO, which said the creation of a new independent tribunal was an essential prerequisite for a fair and effective prison disciplinary system. It pressed the government to implement 'this long overdue reform' without delay. NACRO's fulsome welcome for the Prior Committee's report is perhaps no great surprise – the Director of NACRO, Vivien Stern, was a member of the Prior Committee.

## CRIMINAL INJURIES COMPENSATION BOARD

If you have been injured as the result of a crime of violence, you can apply to the Criminal Injuries Compensation Board for a compensation payment from the government. One man who was very seriously disabled after being attacked was recently awarded more than £120,000. There are various conditions of course, but there's no catch; the Board is so keen to give away money that, for example, within two days of the bomb explosion outside Harrods at the end of 1983 it had delivered a pile of leaflets and application forms to hospitals where the injured were being treated. You too can get a form and leaflet if you need them from the Criminal Injuries Compensation Board, 19 Alfred Place, London WC1E 7EA, telephone 01–636 9501.

The quaint thing about the Board is that although it has now paid out more than £200 million pounds over 21 years, it has no legal existence: it was not created by legislation. It is, according to the Master of the Rolls Sir John Donaldson, 'a servant of the Crown charged by the Crown, by executive instruction, with the duty of distributing the bounty of the Crown'. So nobody has a right to compensation from the Board. It has a discretion to make *ex gratia* grants in accordance with a published scheme. But although it's possible to get judicial review of a decision, you can't sue the Board, because Parliament has not given you a right, as such, to compensation.

However, the Government has now decided that it would be a good idea to have a statutory scheme after all. The Home Office had intended to introduce a Criminal Justice Bill – a portmanteau or rag-bag of bits and pieces – at the end of 1985; legislation to put the criminal injuries scheme on a statutory basis was to have been included. But the Bill was postponed for a year: the plan now is to introduce it at the end of 1986 in the hope of getting it through by the summer of 1987.

Meanwhile the Board simply gets on with the job of handing out money. You can apply for compensation if you were injured

* As a result of a crime of violence (which can include arson or poisoning).
* When you were trying to stop someone from committing a crime.
* When you were trying to apprehend a suspect after a crime.
* When you were trying to help the police apprehend someone.

You can also apply for compensation if you are the widow or widower of someone who died from criminal injuries, or who was injured but died from some other cause. Other close relatives and dependants may also have a claim. If you are not a relative or dependant of the victim but you paid towards the funeral, you can claim reasonable expenses.

You can apply for compensation even if the injuries were caused by someone who could not be held responsible under the criminal law, for example because they were too young or were insane. You can also apply even if the person who committed the crime is not known or has not been brought to justice.

You must apply within three years of the date you were injured. The Board will not make an exception to this rule unless there are very special circumstances.

Compensation is assessed by the Board in the same way that the courts assess damages. It's usually paid as a lump sum by cheque. But, as we've said, there are some conditions.

The Board doesn't want to be bothered with trivial injuries and won't make any payment at all if the appropriate compensation is less than £400. Injuries caused by traffic accidents are not normally covered. The Board may withhold or reduce compensation if you've not told the police and not helped bring the offender to justice.

You must be able to convince the Board that you were not responsible in any way for the incident in which you were injured. Otherwise the Board may decide that they cannot make a full award, or any award at all. The Board may also take into account your character and way of life.

Some of the conditions are different if you and the person who injured you were living together as members of the same family. (A man and a woman living together as husband and wife, even if they are not married, are members of the same family.) In such cases the injury must be serious enough for the Board to award compensation of at least £500; the person who injured you must have been prosecuted (unless there are good reasons why this cannot be done); and you and the person who injured you must have stopped living together. (This condition does not apply if it was a child who was injured.)

As we've said, if you want to apply for compensation you have to fill in a form. It's quite long and detailed, but well printed and clearly laid out. The information you give will be checked; fraudulent applicants are prosecuted. You will have to sign a section at the end of the form which gives the Board permission to write to the police, your doctor, your employer, or other people to confirm what you have said about your injuries and loss of earnings. All these enquiries are dealt with in strict confidence.

If you've made an application, one of these Board members will decide whether your case is covered by the Scheme and, if it is, how much compensation you should be awarded. You will be informed of the decision. If you are not satisfied with the decision, you can ask for a hearing.

At a hearing, three other members of the Board look at the case afresh. They may decide to make an award even if the Board member who looked at the case earlier did not do so. Or they may reject your application although an award was made earlier. Or they may increase or reduce the award.

Hearings are held in private and are as informal as possible. You have to provide whatever evidence is necessary, and arrange for any witnesses you want to call to be present. The Board will give what help it can, if you ask. You can bring a friend or legal adviser to help, but the Board will not pay legal costs. You may be able to claim reasonable expenses for yourself and your witnesses.

Deductions are made from an award of compensation to cover social security payments; pension arrangements made by your employer; certain insurance policies; and any other compensation you may receive from the courts or elsewhere.

More than 21,000 people received compensation during the

year 1983/84, amounting to nearly £33 million in all. The Board's annual reports give an idea of how much compensation you might get for certain types of injury.

## DISCRIMINATION

Discrimination on grounds of sex or race is, in general, unlawful. By 'unlawful' we mean you can take action in the civil courts to prevent it, or to get compensation. Discrimination is not, as such, illegal: it's not a criminal offence.

### Sex discrimination in general

There are two Acts of Parliament dealing with sex discrimination, the Equal Pay Act 1970 and the Sex Discrimination Act 1975. Both took effect at the end of 1975, but the Equal Pay Act was amended with effect from 1984 by regulations designed to bring it into line with European law, as declared by the European Court of Justice at Luxembourg in 1982.

The Equal Pay Act gives you rights relating to your contract of employment. The Sex Discrimination Act relates to discrimination on grounds of sex or marriage in non-contractual matters.

The Sex Discrimination Act set up a public body known as the Equal Opportunities Commission (EOC). It has a duty to work towards the elimination of discrimination, to promote equal opportunities between the sexes and to keep under review the working of the Sex Discrimination Act and the Equal Pay Act. It sees one of its most important roles as advising people of their rights under the two Acts, and thus encouraging people to exercise them. In addition the EOC sometimes helps people take cases to a court or tribunal by instructing and paying the lawyers, generally in cases which raise a question of principle. But even if you only want their leaflets it's worth getting in touch with the Equal Opportunities Commission as soon as possible. Their address is

Overseas House, Quay Street, Manchester M3 3HN, telephone 061–833 9244.

## The Equal Pay Act

The purpose of the Equal Pay Act is to eliminate discrimination between men and women in basic rates of pay and other terms of their employment contracts, such as overtime payments, working hours, holidays and sick leave entitlement.

There are now three grounds on which you can claim equal pay to that of a man. (The Act applies to both men and women of course, but as it's usually women who claim equal pay with men we'll assume for the purposes of this chapter that you, dear reader, are a woman.) The first ground applies if you are doing 'like work' – the same or broadly similar work to that of a man. The second ground applies where your job has been rated the same under a 'job evaluation study'. The third ground (and this is the new one) applies where you are doing work of 'equal value' to that of a man in the same employment in terms of the demands made (under such headings as effort, skill, and decision-making).

The chances are that the first two categories won't be much use to you. That's because most cases where a woman could show she was doing the same job as a man had been settled within three or four years of the Equal Pay Act coming into force. The EOC points out this doesn't mean most women had achieved equal pay – merely that most women workers were doing jobs that were never done by men, so there was nobody to compare themselves with.

Since the law was changed in 1984 over 200 women workers have claimed equal pay for work of equal value. The first successful case was brought by Julie Hayward, a catering worker paid £99 a week, who said her work at a shipyard canteen was of equal worth, and demanded equal skill and responsibility, as the jobs of painters, joiners, and thermal heating engineers who were paid £130 a week. But she then ran into further difficulties when the shipyard, Cammell Laird, refused to increase her wages by the full amount she'd claimed, as they said she had other benefits which the manual workers didn't get.

Claims for equal pay are made to an industrial tribunal – a relatively informal sort of court. You can apply at any time while you are doing the job in question or up to six months after you leave. You have to fill in a form (IT1) which you send to the Central Office of Industrial Tribunals (93 Ebury Bridge Road, London SW1, tel. 01–730 9161). The Conciliation Service ACAS will then step in to see if the dispute between you and your employer can be settled without the need for a hearing. But if you do win your case at a tribunal, your employer can be ordered to pay you at the same rate as a comparable man in future. You can also get two years' back pay. It's possible to appeal to the Employment Appeal Tribunal on a point of law, and from there to the Court of Appeal.

## The Sex Discrimination Act

The Sex Discrimination Act makes sex discrimination unlawful in employment; education; the provision of housing, goods, facilities and services; and advertising. Again the Act applies equally to men and women, but as it's usually women who are discriminated against we'll continue to assume that you, the reader, are a woman.

There are two kinds of sex discrimination. 'Direct discrimination' involves treating a woman less favourably than a man because she is a woman. 'Indirect discrimination' means imposing unjustifiable conditions which fewer women are able to meet than men.

The example given by the EOC is of an employer who insists on recruiting staff at least six feet tall. This is not direct discrimination because the job is not restricted to men. But it could be indirect discrimination because it's more likely that men will be able to meet the qualifications.

As we've said, sex discrimination is not allowed in the field of employment. In addition, it's also unlawful to discriminate in employment against someone who's married. Discrimination on marital grounds is allowed outside the area of employment, so long as it doesn't amount to unlawful sex discrimination (or race discrimination – see later). Direct discrimination against a married person means treating him or her less favourably than an unmarried person of the same sex, because that person is married. Indirect discrimination against a married person means imposing unjustifiable conditions which fewer married people are able to meet than unmarried people of the same sex.

Employers may not discriminate in their recruitment or treatment of you because you are married or a woman. This does not apply to people who work in private households, or to employers who have not more than five staff. Sex discrimination is also not unlawful where a person's sex is a 'genuine occupational qualification' for the job. Eight examples of this are given in the Act so here, as throughout this book, it's worth reading the small print if you think it may affect you. There are other exceptions. And don't forget, as we've just seen, that the Equal Pay Act also deals with employment.

Co-educational schools, colleges and universities may not discriminate on grounds of sex in admissions or the facilities they provide. In 1984 Bromley Council in South London and the former head teacher of a primary school in the borough admitted discrimination against three twelve-year-old schoolgirls who'd been held back a year because of their sex. Each girl got £350 compensation.

Sex discrimination by anyone providing goods, facilities or services is unlawful. This covers access to public places, hotel accommodation, banking, insurance, entertainment, restaurants, travel and professional services. There are exceptions for such things as private clubs and to preserve decency and privacy. Insurers are entitled to discriminate on the basis of actuarial information: in 1985 a woman lost her case against a life insurance company, which charged women higher premiums than men for health cover, because the court found a substantial loading against women was justified by the statistics.

The insurance exception applies throughout the Act. Other general exceptions relate to charities, sports, statutory requirements, and communal accommodation.

If you feel you've been the victim of discrimination, you can take legal action. Complaints in the field of employment are made to industrial tribunals, which use the procedure we mentioned in the previous section. There is a three month time limit. Complaints in other areas of discrimination are heard in the county court, with a right of appeal to the Court of Appeal. The county court time limit is six months.

In addition, the Equal Opportunities Commission itself can carry out formal investigations. If it finds the Sex Discrimination Act or the Equal Pay Act has been broken, it can serve a non-discrimination notice on the person concerned, telling him to stop. A court may grant an injunction to stop persistent discrimination.

Only the EOC can take proceedings against discriminatory advertisements – those which indicate an intention to discriminate unlawfully. So an advertisement for, say, a waiter must make it clear that the job is open to men and women (unless the advertiser can rely on an exception such as a genuine occupational qualification). But there is nothing the Equal Opportunities Commission can do about sexist product advertising, and they say their complaints about this to the Advertising Standards Authority (which of course is not, in the legal sense, an authority at all) have not been upheld because the advertisements were said not to give 'grave' or 'widespread' offence.

The EOC is also empowered to issue codes of practice. The first code on equal opportunity policies, procedures and practices was published in 1985. Though approved by Parliament it's not legally binding. But, rather like the Highway Code, failure to comply with it can be used in evidence at an industrial tribunal. It gives guidelines on the Sex Discrimination Act reflecting current attitudes, practices and policies.

## Racial discrimination in general

The law on racial discrimination is in many ways similar to the sex discrimination law we've just described. Racial discrimination was made unlawful by the Race Relations Act 1976, and in the rest of this chapter we'll explain what this means. The Act set up a

129

body called the Commission for Racial Equality (CRE). Its address is Elliot House, 10–12 Allington Street, London SW1E 5EH, telephone 01–828 7022. The Commission for Racial Equality (or CRE) also has regional offices in Birmingham, Manchester, Leicester and Leeds. We'll be discussing its work in more detail later.

## The Race Relations Act

There are again two types of discrimination prohibited by the Act, direct and indirect.

'Direct racial discrimination' arises where a person treats another person less favourably on 'racial grounds' than he treats, or would treat, someone else. Racial grounds cover colour, race, nationality (which includes citizenship) or ethnic or national origins. The Act does not prohibit discrimination on religious grounds as such, but some forms of religious discrimination may be covered by the prohibition of discrimination against people on the basis of their ethnic origins. The Commission for Racial Equality says a decision of the House of Lords in the case of *Mandla v. Dowell-Lee* in 1983 'reveals the close connection between religion and ethnicity, and shows that the present Race Relations Act offers considerable assistance where the religion's practice is a cultural norm associated with the ethnic group as in the case of Muslims, Sikhs and Jews'. It says the government should now consider whether religious discrimination should be made unlawful.

The CRE points out that a person's motives for discriminating are irrelevant. Somebody who refused to appoint black people to work in a shop because of customer resistance would still be breaking the law even if he personally had no objections to black staff. Although it may be necessary to examine someone's motives to see if he was discriminating on racial grounds, it is the existence of the racial grounds that is the test, not the existence of a racial motive as such.

'Indirect racial discrimination' consists of applying a requirement or condition which, whether intentionally or not, adversely affects one racial group considerably more than another and cannot be justified on non-racial grounds. The CRE says that to require a high standard of English from a labourer might be considered unlawful if the effect were to exclude members of any racial group who had limited English but could do the job. The CRE would like to see this definition strengthened.

'Discrimination by means of victimisation' is also made unlawful. The aim is to protect people who've made complaints under the Act; the CRE would like this definition improved too.

The Act makes racial discrimination unlawful in employment and training, in education, in the provision of goods, facilities and services, and in housing. We'll look at each of these in turn.

## Employment

Generally, an employer must not discriminate in the arrangements he makes for selecting employees, either in the terms on which he offers employment, or by refusing or deliberately omitting to offer a person employment.

An employment agency must not normally discriminate in providing its services – for example, in submitting applicants to employers, giving information about available jobs, or advising applicants on jobs or careers.

A body or authority which grants qualifications or authorisation to carry on a trade or profession must not discriminate in doing so.

An employer normally must not discriminate in allowing his employees access to opportunities for training, promotion, or transfer to other jobs; in the terms and conditions of employment he affords his employees; or in providing access to any other benefit. He must not, on racial grounds, dismiss an employee or subject him to any other unfavourable treatment.

Generally, training bodies must not discriminate in the provision of facilities for training, selection of applicants for training, or treatment of trainees.

A trade union must not discriminate in granting

131

membership; in the terms of conditions of membership; in providing services to members; or by terminating a person's membership or subjecting him to any unfavourable treatment.

There are inevitably exceptions. You'll remember the 'genuine occupational qualification' from the Sex Discrimination Act. Sure enough, racial discrimination is not unlawful where membership of a particular racial group is a genuine occupational qualification for a job; or where the employment is for the purpose of training an overseas resident in skills to be used overseas; or where the employment is in a private household. In addition, special steps are permitted where the purpose is to train persons of a particular racial group for employment where that group is under-represented, or to encourage them to seek such employment.

## Education

Schools, colleges and universities must not discriminate in the admission or treatment of students. There is a general exception, which applies to training, welfare or ancillary benefits as well as education: it allows access to facilities, services or benefits to be restricted, or to be allocated first, to members of a particular racial group if they have special needs (for example, if special provision for teaching English is needed).

## Goods and services

It is unlawful for anyone who provides goods, facilities and services to the public to discriminate against any client or customer. This covers, for example, shops; restaurants and public houses; insurance companies; building societies; car rental firms; doctors; government departments and local authorities; and many other organisations.

## Housing

It is unlawful for anyone selling property to discriminate in choosing a buyer, or in the terms on which he sells it. The only exception is for an owner who wholly occupies the property, and who does not advertise it for sale or sell it through an estate agent.

A landlord must not discriminate in letting accommodation. The only exception to this is where a landlord or his close relative lives on the premises and shares facilities with tenants and there is room for only two households or up to six individuals in addition to the landlord and his relative. A landlord must not discriminate in the way he treats tenants.

Estate agents and accommodation agencies must not discriminate in providing services to clients by, for example, not telling clients of suitable properties on the market, unless the property is covered by an exception.

Business premises and land are also covered by the Act.

## Other forms of discrimination

It is unlawful for a club with 25 or more members to discriminate in admitting applicants to membership, or in its treatment of members. An exception is for clubs whose essential purpose is to enable the benefits of membership to be enjoyed by persons of a particular racial group (though not persons selected on grounds of colour).

It is unlawful for anyone to instruct, or attempt to induce, or help someone to discriminate. And it's normally unlawful to publish an advertisement or notice which indicates an intention to discriminate. Only the CRE may bring proceedings in these cases.

## Positive action

The law does not allow 'reverse discrimination': you're not allowed to discriminate against white people to help black people, for example. But certain types of 'positive action' are permitted: where a particular racial group is 'under-represented' in any work at an establishment, the employer may afford only employees of that racial group access to training to help fit them for the work; or encourage only members of that racial group to take advantage of opportunities to do the work.

133

A racial group can be counted as under-represented if, at any time during the previous twelve months, either there was no one of that group doing the work in question; or there were disproportionately few in comparison with the group's proportion in the work force as a whole at that establishment, or in the relevant labour market.

Training bodies may similarly discriminate in providing training for particular work, or encouraging people to enter the work, in the case of any racial group under-represented in that work either in Great Britain as a whole or any part of Great Britain.

A trade union may provide training for posts within the union only to members of the union who are of a particular racial group, or encourage only such members to take advantage of opportunities for such posts, where that racial group is under-represented in those posts compared with its proportion in the membership. A union may also encourage only persons of a particular racial group to become members if that racial group is under-represented in the membership compared with their proportion among those eligible for membership.

There's also a general exception to the Act if discrimination occurs in selecting someone for a place on a sports team.

## Remedies

As with sex discrimination, complaints of racial discrimination in employment can be made to an industrial tribunal. Normally, you must make your complaint within three months of the act complained of (although a tribunal may accept complaints outside this time limit if there are very special reasons for doing so). If a hearing is held, and the tribunal upholds your case, it may award the following redress: a declaration of your rights; financial compensation (except where the case concerns indirect discrimination, and the respondent proves this was unintentional); or recommendations to the respondent on action he should take to remedy the effects on the complainant of the discrimination.

Again, a copy of your application to the tribunal is sent to the Conciliation Service ACAS, which has to consider whether the case can be settled without the need for a hearing.

Other complaints (those relating to education, housing, goods, facilities and services) can be heard in one of 16 designated county courts in England and Wales. But the CRE said in 1985 that this procedure has fallen almost into disuse, probably because of the expense and long delays inherent in the procedure. There were only 18 such cases in 1983. The CRE wants to see a discrimination division within the industrial tribunal system to hear both employment and non-employment cases involving sex discrimination or racial discrimination.

## The Commission for Racial Equality

The CRE has the job of working towards the elimination of discrimination; it also has a duty to promote equality of opportunity and good relations between different racial groups.

The CRE helps people who believe that they have been discriminated against and who want to take a case to court or an industrial tribunal. The CRE can give straightforward advice on procedures; it can provide a lawyer to represent the complainant; it can pay solicitors' costs; and, in exceptional cases, it can provide a barrister.

So just as your first step in a sex discrimination case should be to contact the Equal Opportunities Commission, you should get in touch with the Commission for Racial Equality (whose address we gave earlier) if you need help or advice on racial discrimination. But the CRE's funds are limited, and so it has urged the government to provide legal aid for cases involving racial discrimination heard by industrial tribunals.

The CRE also has powers to conduct formal investigations. For example, it can investigate the recruitment practices of a firm which employs a small number of black employees in relation to the make-up of the local community. Where it finds discrimination, it may issue a non-discrimination notice requiring this to cease, which becomes binding unless quashed or revised on appeal. It may conduct further investigations within five years to verify compliance with the notice. It may bring proceedings for an injunction or order against persistent discriminators. However, the value of the power to conduct formal investigations has been diminished by a decision of the House of Lords in 1984 which interpreted a section of the Act in a restrictive way. It now seems that it will no longer be possible for the CRE to carry out formal investigations of a strategic nature into such areas as housing, education or employment unless information is obtained before the investigation which leads the CRE to believe that discrimination is occurring, or unless the investigation has wide-ranging general terms of reference. The CRE says it will now be more difficult to use investigations to uncover systems and procedures which cause indirect and often unintended discrimination. Not surprisingly, it want the House of Lords' decision reversed by Parliament.

The CRE has issued a Code of Practice for the elimination of racial discrimination and the promotion of equality of opportunity in employment. This has been passed by Parliament. The Code is a set of recommendations and guidance on how racial discrimination in employment can be avoided. It contains general advice on the policies that are needed, and detailed recommendations, for example, on ways of preventing discrimination in the recruitment and treatment of employees as well as outlining those steps which can have a positive impact on equal opportunity. At present the CRE is not able to issue codes relating to other types of racial discrimination: it would like to have that power.

The CRE can give money to organisations who provide advice and counselling to ethnic minorities and who are concerned with improving race relations. Money is available for youth training schemes, employment projects, advice centres, educational facilities, ethnic minority art and facilities for elderly members of ethnic minorities. The CRE's funds are limited and money is usually used to help new schemes to get off the ground.

Community Relations Councils are independent organisations run by local people to meet local needs. The CRE does, however, provide certain staff costs and lays down guidelines on areas of activities. It can also give CRCs additional finance for specific projects. Running costs and other expenses are met by local authorities.

# 4 *The family in society*

Society has grown over the years based on family life. The usual concept of a family is two parents with children who comprise a domestic unit. Increasingly today there are one-parent families, childless families and a good many people who live together as husband and wife without being married.

What are your rights within the family? How do individual rights relate to family responsibilities? What are the rights of children and what are the responsibilities of parents towards their children?

## MARRIAGE

Let's first take marriage. In our western society people are entitled to marry anyone they choose. No one may marry until the age of 16 and then only with parental consent. If the parents of a person between the ages of 16 and 18 are divorced, then it is the parent who has custody of the child who must give that consent. At the age of 18 a marriage can take place without such consent. The parties to a marriage must be of opposite sexes – the law does not recognise a homosexual marriage.

You're not allowed to marry close relatives and of course you're not allowed to have more than one spouse.

### Christian marriage

In order for a valid marriage to take place it must conform with the provisions of the Marriage Act 1949. In this country there is an 'established Church' – the Church of England (and in Wales, the Church in Wales). Any marriage which takes place in another type of church or in a register office requires separate civil proceedings.

A Church of England marriage requires the reading of banns in the parish churches of each of the parties to the wedding on three successive Sundays. The wedding must take place within three months of the final reading.

If the marriage is to take place in a church of a different denomination or in a register office, then a certificate must be obtained from the Superintendent Registrar.

## Other marriages

If you are not getting married in a Church of England ceremony, you need to get a certificate from a register office first. This applies even if you're not getting married in the register office. There are two sorts of certificate. One without a licence allows you to get married 21 days after you have given notice and said that you believe there is no impediment to the marriage. If you and your intended spouse live in different districts you must give notice in each area. A certificate with a licence allows you to get married two days after you give notice (there must be one clear day between the day on which you give notice and the day you marry). To get a certificate with a licence you need to have been living in the district for fifteen days, but only one party to the marriage need give notice.

Once you've got the certificate (with or without a licence) you've then got a choice of places to marry. There is of course the local register office (it has to be the office where one of the parties gave notice, which of course is in the area where he or she lives). There must be no religious ceremony in a register office, but it's then up to you if you want a religious service afterwards. Students sometimes 'get married' in the chapel of a college at Oxford or Cambridge. But unless they've gone to the trouble and expense of getting a special licence from the Archbishop of Canterbury (which allows you to get married anywhere) the normal practice is for the legal marriage to take place in the register office and a religious ceremony to follow.

However, it is possible for the Registrar General to register for marriages any building which is certified as a place of religious worship. The minister of the faith or denomination involved will normally be authorised to conduct the marriage and, whatever other ceremony is involved, a declaration similar to the one used in the register office is required: 'I take thee to be my lawful wedded wife' (or 'husband').

Quakers and Jews have special rights (or privileges). The Society of Friends are allowed to marry people according to their own rules. So too are Jews, provided both parties 'profess the Jewish religion'. In these cases no declaration in the prescribed form is required: in an orthodox Jewish wedding the declaration is in Hebrew. Jews and Quakers are allowed to get married whenever they like; other marriages (without a special licence) have to be between 8 am and 6 pm.

The Registrar General has power to allow people to get married anywhere if one of them is too ill to be moved and not expected to recover.

## The effect of marriage

Once the marriage has taken place there are certain new rights and obligations placed on the spouses. It has been traditional for a wife to change her surname to that of her husband. She has the right to do this, but it is not a legal obligation and indeed, today, many women who have their own careers or professions are choosing to retain their maiden names after marriage. Since people can, on the whole, take whatever name they like, a man can take his wife's name or they can hyphenate the two names together.

There is a duty to inform the Inland Revenue and the DHSS after the wedding as liabilities, allowances, and eligibility for benefits are affected by the fact of marriage.

There are certain other rights and obligations associated with marriage – such as consent to sexual intercourse. In law a man cannot be guilty of raping his wife, although there is pressure from some organisations to change the law so that in some circumstances, even though the parties are married, the wife's consent should not automatically be implied. Divorce or a separation order implies the withdrawal of such consent.

There is an obligation to respect confidences received within marriage, and there is a right not to have to give evidence against the other party to the marriage in a criminal trial.

## BREAKDOWN OF MARRIAGE

We all know of marriages which for some reason have gone wrong. There are now around 150,000 divorces a year compared with around 25,000 in 1960.

Historically, the church courts had control of all marriage disputes and, until comparatively recently, it was necessary to get a special Act of Parliament passed in each individual case in order to obtain a divorce. The first liberalisation came in Victorian times when a husband was allowed to divorce his wife if she had committed adultery. That remained the case until 1937 when an Act was passed allowing divorce if it was proved that there had been cruelty, desertion or adultery. It was necessary to prove any one of these three grounds and there was a great element of establishing guilt in the obtaining of a divorce.

### *The ground for divorce*

In 1969 a private member's Bill went through Parliament abolishing the concept of proving unacceptable conduct in matrimonial matters. That Act substituted the concept of 'irretrievable breakdown of marriage'. Once that has been established, then a divorce may be obtained irrespective of the 'guilt' of either party.

The law today is still based on the irretrievable breakdown of the marriage but, in 1984, the Matrimonial and Family Proceedings Act changed the law in some important respects. Until that Act, it was not generally possible to petition for divorce within three years of marriage (except in some exceptional circumstances).

The new Act introduces an absolute bar on divorce in the first year of the marriage. This follows a Law Commission recommendation. There are no exceptions to this one-year rule, whatever the hardship. Until the passing of this Act, there was a discretion for the courts to allow a petition within the first three years in cases of exceptional hardship or depravity. Now the position is that there may not be a petition at all within 12 months of the marriage but that matters occurring within that year may be relied upon if a petition is presented after that period.

The law recognises, however, that there may be intolerable situations arising within a marriage from day one. It is possible to apply to the court for a decree of judicial separation for which there is no time bar at all. The effect of that order is the same as divorce, except it does not allow re-marriage. Divorce is the complete untangling of the legal contract of marriage, but a husband and wife who have obtained an order of judicial separation are not free to re-marry. It may therefore be attractive for people who have religious objections to divorce. To get a judicial separation you have to prove one of the five 'reasons' for divorce mentioned in the next section.

The Law Commission has found that these orders are being used as a short-term measure pending divorce and most people in this situation eventually ask for and obtain a divorce. Judicial separation is sometimes used as a bargaining counter to extract an improved settlement from a husband in exchange for his freedom. That's because the granting of an order for judicial separation entitles the court to look at the financial position of the parties in the same way as it does in a divorce case. Orders can be made for maintenance or a lump sum payment, for property adjustments, and for the future care of any children of the family.

## How to be divorced

Let's now look at how to get a divorce. We have already explained the one-year rule and we must now examine the meaning of irretrievable breakdown of marriage. Society now accepts that in such a situation it is better for the marriage to be ended so that

141

both partners can build a new life for themselves. There are, broadly speaking, five reasons which the court will accept as evidence that this state of affairs had occurred. They are first that the husband and wife have been living apart for two years and both consent to the divorce; secondly that one spouse has deserted the other for at least two years (this is now a rarely used ground for divorce); thirdly that the husband and wife have lived apart for at least five years (no consent to the divorce is required from the other spouse after this time); fourthly, that the husband or wife has committed adultery and the other party to the marriage finds it intolerable to continue living with him or her; and finally that the husband or wife has behaved unreasonably. This last ground for divorce is fairly wide and there is no accurate definition of it. It allows divorce to be granted where it is intolerable to expect the parties to continue to live together; and it will generally depend on all the facts in each particular case as to whether the circumstances of the breakdown of the marriage amount to unreasonable behaviour.

The courts have held that such things as verbal and physical abuse; financial irresponsibility; drink or drug problems; refusal to have children; gambling; and refusal to maintain the other spouse are all matters which amount to unreasonable behaviour.

## Money after a divorce

Once the court is satisfied that there are grounds for divorce as outlined above, then a decree nisi will be granted. This does not mean that the parties are yet divorced as there are generally a number of matters to be sorted out, including financial arrangements and arrangements for any children in the family. Only after these have been sorted out to the satisfaction of the court will a decree absolute (the actual divorce) be granted. It is here that the new Matrimonial and Family Proceedings Act 1984 changes the law considerably. The main thrust of this Act relates to financial provision after divorce and the new emphasis is that first consideration should be given to the needs of any children of the family.

The idealistic aim of any financial settlement is to put both parties in as similar a financial position as possible to what they would have been in had the marriage not ended. Alas, this is rarely possible in the majority of cases and the Act removes the obligation on the court to try and achieve it. The new Act allows the court to look at the conduct of the parties if it deems it appropriate. This is one of the more controversial aspects of the Act and initially many people regarded it as a retrograde step towards the old philosophy of guilt by one or other of the parties to the divorce. But so far conduct does not seem to have figured more prominently under the new law. The 1984 Act also recognises the advantages of making a clean break on divorce where at all possible. This will, of course, greatly depend on whether there are children and also the employability and income of the wife. There is, however, a specific provision for the court to consider whether maintenance for a wife can be ordered to terminate after a certain period of time allowing a 'rehabilitation period' for the parties to adjust to their new-found independence.

What, therefore, will the court look at when considering how the financial cake will be divided on divorce? There is always a discretion in the court to look at the particular facts and circumstances in each case. After all, nobody's circumstances are the same as anyone else's and it would be foolish to assume that they were.

When an application is made to the court for financial provision, an affidavit has to be sworn setting out the exact details of income and capital so that the registrar can see exactly what resources are available for division. The earning capacity of each of the parties will be considered, but the courts try to deal with the reality of what is available rather than what should theoretically be available. It is of course open to the parties to come to an agreement on money matters and indeed the court will usually welcome this, as what is done voluntarily is more likely to be problem-free than what is done under a court order.

When considering what provision should be made for any relevant children the court may order specific regular payments to the children or a lump sum payment. The court will also wish to be satisfied that the parent who has custody of the children has a proper home in which to bring them up and will want to ensure that there is enough money for rent or mortgage payments to be made.

The court will look at the child as an individual and try to assess its financial needs, taking into account its education, its income or earning capacity, and any mental or physical disability from which it suffers. Maintenance for a child usually continues until the age of 18 or until the child ceases to be in full-time education.

## Violent spouses

One reads increasingly these days of reports of violence within marriage. What rights are there for a spouse who is being subjected to violence and abuse? It is possible to obtain an injunction from the court ordering the molestation to stop, or ordering the violent spouse out of the matrimonial home. The courts are, however, becoming more reluctant to use an exclusion order. It is possible since the Domestic Violence and Matrimonial Proceedings Act of 1976 for the court to issue an injunction whether or not there are divorce proceedings pending, and the order may refer to violence towards the other spouse or any child of the family. The court can also order one party to allow the other into all or part of the matrimonial home.

## Common law marriage?

Let's now turn to the increasingly common incidence of people living together in stable and long-term relationships who are not actually married. These arrangements are popularly known as 'common law relationships'; 'common law husband' and 'common law wife' are phrases often heard in conversation or used by the newspapers. However, these phrases have no legal meaning at all and their use confers no rights on the individuals concerned. (They're also sometimes called 'cohabitees': we prefer the word 'cohabitant'.)

The law in some respects is slow to follow the social evolution of such relationships and although the woman may be able to claim maintenance for children of such a family from the natural father, she will not obtain maintenance for herself. It is only in exceptional cases that she will be able to claim a share of the house in which the couple live if it is in the man's name; and in this situation she runs the risk of being evicted if the relationship goes wrong. The strict interpretation of this is that as no marriage has taken place, then it cannot be presumed that the property belongs to the 'family'. Normally the owner of the property will have all the rights over it.

There are, though, some circumstances where the property might be regarded as jointly owned, but these are strictly limited. For instance, if the non-owner provided the deposit for the house and paid the mortgage, or has done a lot of work on the property, the court may regard it as jointly owned. However, it is difficult to prove all this to the satisfaction of the courts and you should not assume that judges will make orders along these lines.

If the couple bought the house and put it in joint names, then it will normally be divided equally if the relationship ends. If the couple occupy rented property, then the rights for the person whose name is not on the rent book are limited. If the couple are married, it is possible for the court to transfer the tenancy from husband to wife or vice versa. If they are not married then the tenancy cannot be transferred and must be allowed to remain with the original tenant. An abandoned cohabitant whose name is not on the rent book or lease has no right to remain there, except with the agreement of the landlord, and will run the risk of eviction. Such a relationship may also have implications for any children. These are dealt with under the section on illegitimacy on page 158.

## Rights and responsibilities in marriage

You can see that marriage confers certain rights and responsibilities on the parties to the marriage and their children. Rights on the breakdown of a relationship have recently changed. The so called 'meal ticket for life' has gone as a concept and the criteria for assessing financial relief have changed. It seems likely that as the new law evolves in practice, the courts will consider the desirability of a clean break, making the financial settlement a 'one-off' provision instead of a continuing obligation between the parties. It is too early yet to analyse decisions of the courts in such cases, but it seems likely that the new emphasis will lead to a reallocation of capital assets – the wife for example being provided with a cash lump-sum while the matrimonial home is sold and the proceeds divided. Regular weekly or monthly payments would not be ordered if a clean break was the aim, to avoid a continuing obligation between the former spouses.

It will be interesting to see how the courts apply the provisions of the new Matrimonial and Family Proceedings Act 1984, as judges are often unpredictable in their interpretation of statutes. Another interesting exercise will be to assess how the courts are reacting to their newly-revived apparent power to look at matters of conduct arising from the marriage. The key phrase in the new Act is that the court should have regard to the conduct of the parties if in the opinion of the court 'it would be inequitable to disregard it'. Some lawyers maintain that this will now make conduct a feature of divorce proceedings though it is too early to prove this. But it seems that in many cases arguments over money, which are already often very bitter and distressingly protracted, will become more so as each party tries to raise matters of conduct within the marriage in order to increase or decrease any financial provision which the court might order.

## FAMILY COURTS

There is one other area of family law where reform is overdue – the system of courts which deal with matrimonial and family matters. At present there are as many as three different sorts of court which can have jurisdiction over one broken marriage. There is increasing pressure on the government to review and reform the system so that all disputes relating to the family are dealt with by one Family Court. Let's look at the background to this.

There has been a growing campaign over the past few years both from individual lawyers and larger organisations for the setting up of a Family Court in place of the present arrangements. The Finer Committee on One-Parent Families in 1974 set out these criteria for a family court:

* It should be an impartial judicial institution, regulating the rights of citizens and settling their disputes according to law;

* It should apply a uniform set of legal rules derived from a single moral standard and applicable to all citizens;

* It should organise its work in such a way as to provide the best possible facilities for conciliation between parties in matrimonial disputes;

* It would have professionally trained staff to assist both the court and the parties appearing before it in all matters requiring social work services and advice;

* It would work in close relationship with the social security authorities in the assessment both of need and of liability in cases involving financial provision; and

* It would organise its procedure, sittings and administrative services and arrangements with a view to gaining the confidence and maximising the convenience of the citizens who appear before it.

At present, there are three separate courts with jurisdiction in family matters – the magistrates' court, the county court, and the High Court Family Division. In addition there are further courts to hear appeals. This combination of jurisdictions is a historical accident; each of the courts is of a very different character; and the distribution of business between them has been described as 'chaotic'.

There is an overlap in jurisdiction, particularly between the magistrates' domestic court and the county court. This inevitably results in two systems of family law being administered in two different types of court. This division of powers between the courts is far from satisfactory and it is worth looking again at the Finer Committee Report, which said:

> A family crisis is seldom simple and it is highly desirable that the court dealing with it has a wide range of powers at its disposal. In a given situation orders relating to cash support, occupation of the home, ownership of family assets and the custody of children might be necessary in order to deal with the situation as a whole. The orders relate to and supplement each other. It is quite wrong that a spouse for whom all those orders may be appropriate must seek them from different courts, differently constituted, using their own characteristic procedures and sitting according to their own individual time schedules.

Further confusion is often caused by the fact that neither the county court nor the magistrates' court has jurisdiction exclusively in family matters. The magistrates' courts are seen as criminal courts, whereas the county courts deal with the full range of civil disputes.

Many people believe that it would be important to ensure that care proceedings in the juvenile court are brought into the Family Court. These are not criminal proceedings, but civil proceedings between (usually) the local authority on one hand, and the child or its parents (or both) on the other. At present they are dealt with by the juvenile bench in the magistrates' court and are often heard in the same list as criminal matters. They arguably belong more easily in a court which has total jurisdiction in matters relating to children, including custody, guardianship, and adoption.

The proposed Family Court would deal exclusively with all decision-making in family law matters apart from appeals. It would incorporate the Family Division of the High Court, the county court family jurisdiction, the magistrates' court's domestic jurisdiction including the collection and enforcement of maintenance payments, Juvenile Court Care proceedings and Crown

Court appeals against decisions of the magistrates' court in family matters.

A Family Court would provide an effective system for the collection and enforcement of maintenance. Research has been carried out to examine the current methods of collection and enforcement of maintenance with the object of finding the most suitable and efficient system. Family maintenance is a special type of debt and there are arguments for saying that the enforcing officer should be attached to a Family Court. Some provision would have to be made for a Family Court Welfare Service. The British Association of Social Workers has recommended that there should be such a service which would not be part of either the probation service or the local authority social services department. It would be administered by the Family Court and staffed with qualified social workers with several years of experience of work with families and children either in the probation service, or a local authority social services department, or an education department, or in the voluntary sector. The Association argues that such a service would have two sections, one providing independent reports to the court in matrimonial, care and adoption cases and the other acting as a conciliation service which would be available to families who apply themselves or are referred by a solicitor or the court. It recommends that there should be a statutory duty on the court to ensure that a conciliation service is available.

All these ideas were formally considered at an open meeting of lawyers, judges, social work groups and people with experience of matrimonial disputes organised by The Law Society in May 1985. That meeting showed a considerable strength of feeling in favour of a family court as a sensible and logical way of dealing with family matters. It was recognised that any formal legislation was probably some years away, but as pressure continues to grow in favour of a more conciliatory method of dealing with such disputes, we may well see this area of the law changing over the next few years.

# CHILDREN

Most children today are born within the context of a marriage and the next section deals with the rights of children and the responsibilities of parents towards their children.

## Rights of children: the Gillick case

The age of majority is now 18. Anyone under that age is classed as a minor. What rights does a minor have? The answer is that rights and the consequent duties increase as the child gets nearer to adulthood. To balance this, the parents of a child have obligations and duties towards him or her.

This analysis of the law is supported by the majority decision of the House of Lords in the *Gillick* case (though we wrote it before the Lords gave their judgments on the case in October 1985). In Mrs Victoria Gillick's case the three law lords who delivered the majority decision said Mrs Gillick was wrong in claiming that parents had the legal right to stop children under 16 being given contraceptives; they also dismissed her claim that no under-age girl could consent to contraception. They rejected the reliance of the Court of Appeal, when it considered the case, on a nineteenth-century judgment which reflected the Victorians' attitude to children, and the law lords looked through the old law books for a principle which could be applied to the needs of a modern society. That principle, according to Lord Scarman, was that a parent's rights exist only for as long as they are needed to protect a child. He agreed with Lord Fraser of Tullybelton, who thought a doctor was sometimes a better judge than a parent of what was best for a child. In Lord Fraser's view, a doctor could prescribe contraceptives without the parents' consent, or even knowledge, so long as he was satisfied that the girl would understand the advice, that she couldn't be persuaded to let her parents know, that she was likely to have sex anyway, that without contraceptives her health would suffer, and that it was in the girl's best interests. Lord Scarman added that an under-age girl could consent to contraception only if she was mature enough to understand what was involved.

The Children's Legal Centre (20 Compton Terrace, London N1 2UN, telephone 01–359 6251) is an independent national organisation which is concerned with law and policy affecting children and young people in England and Wales. In an excellent *Briefing* on the Gillick case (at £1 only a quarter of the price of the judgment) the Centre sees the Gillick judgment as having three important consequences.

First, it says, parental powers are for the protection of the child. The law lords agreed that parental powers do not stand alone. They spring from a parent's duty towards the child and are given to parents to enable them to carry out their duties.

Secondly, the *Briefing* says, parental powers dwindle as the child matures. It follows from the first point that as a child grows older, he or she is able to take greater responsibility and to make more important decisions. The parents' protective role diminishes. As Lord Denning put it (in 1969), 'parents' rights are dwindling rights'; parental power 'starts with a right of control and ends with little more than advice'.

The third consequence identified by the Children's Legal Centre is that parental powers depend on the understanding of the individual child – they do not cease at any fixed age. The law lords recognised that the control which a parent exercises over a child will vary from child to child and from time to time in the life of any individual child.

Giving judgment in the House of Lords, Lord Fraser and Lord Scarman acknowledged that they were giving wide responsibilities to doctors, but noted that doctors were governed by strict rules and could be disciplined if they abused their powers. The effect of the lords' ruling was to do away with both declarations made by three judges in the Court of Appeal in 1984. One declaration had said the Department of Health's guidance to doctors – which said that in exceptional cases the decision to prescribe contraception was a matter for the clinical judgment of a doctor – was unlawful. The other declaration had been designed to stop Mrs Gillick's own children from being given contraceptives. The House of Lords reached its decision by the narrowest possible majority; the remaining two judges would have rejected the department's guidance – Lord Brandon of Oakbrook, for example, thought that prescribing contraceptives to under-age girls would encourage them to have sex.

## Reasonable parents and reasonable children

Every parent has a legal duty to maintain their child. The standard which is applied throughout is that of a 'reasonable parent'. There is an obligation to look after the child and prevent injury or harm to it. Deliberate violence towards a child will obviously result in criminal charges against the parent and ultimately even the taking of the child into care by the local authority. However, every child deserves a spanking from time to time and the law allows what is called 'reasonable chastisement' of a child. Again the test is one of reasonableness and, as in so many other areas of the law, it is necessary to look at what would commonly be regarded as normal parental behaviour.

## Educational rights of children

As every parent knows, there is an obligation to educate a child. This means there is also a right of the child to receive education. The principal Act governing this is the Education Act 1944. This places not only a duty on the parent, but a duty on the local authority to provide suitable schools to which children may be sent. Every child between the ages of 5 and 16 must be sent to school or receive suitable education. This may mean that a tutor can be employed by the parents at home but the local education authority will have to be satisfied that the child is receiving proper teaching.

The penalty for not educating a child can be a fine of up to £400 or 1 month's imprisonment or both. (The penalty does not apply if a child is ill, or if a child accompanies its family on holiday for up to 2 weeks in any school year.) The local authority may also bring care proceedings.

Parents have the right to choose a school for their child. That school does not have to be the nearest one to the home. If a child is refused admission to a school of the parent's choice then there is the right of appeal to the Local Education Authority. These authorities must now establish Appeal Committees to which parents may appeal within a specified period after refusal. The findings of the Appeal Committee are binding on the Education Authority, although parents have an additional right of appeal to the Secretary of State for Education.

At school, teachers are *in loco parentis* (in the place of a parent) during the time when children are in their charge and therefore have the rights and responsibilities of parents during that time. They must exercise a certain standard of care for the welfare and safety of the child. That standard is accepted by the courts as that of a prudent parent. Broadly this requires a degree of care which does not stifle the natural exuberance or spirit of adventure of the child but would prevent him or her from acting stupidly.

As regards punishment at school, we are all familiar with the school stories where pupils are beaten by the headmaster. The law says that the Head Teacher, being *in loco parentis*, or any teacher to whom he delegates power, has the right to chastise a pupil in a reasonable manner, whether that be by corporal punishment or another form of discipline.

In 1984 a Bill was introduced in Parliament to enable Britain to comply with a European Court of Human Rights ruling in 1982, which said that parents must have their philosophical convictions against corporal punishment respected. It was defeated in the House of Lords and withdrawn, but the government decided later to reintroduce it in the 1985/86 session of Parliament. The Bill would give parents the right to choose whether their children should receive corporal punishment.

The school day at a state school must, under the Education Act, begin with an act of collective worship for all pupils except those who have been withdrawn from such worship by their parents. Any parent who requests that their child should not attend religious worship in school must have that request granted. The religious worship in a state school must not be distinctive of any particular denomination.

153

As distinct from this act of worship, religious instruction in accordance with an agreed syllabus must be given. The syllabus was adopted after the recommendations of a statutory conference of appointed representatives of religious denominations, teachers, and local authorities. Religious education in state schools must therefore not include the teaching of any catechism or belief that is distinctive of any particular religious denomination.

A parent has the right to withdraw his child from religious instruction in the same way as for the daily religious worship.

Some state schools, however, exist as denominational schools and here these rules do not apply: the character of the religious instruction and worship is under the control of the school governors and in accordance with the trust deed relating to that particular school.

## Medical rights of children

If a child becomes ill the parent again has a duty to behave reasonably. If a reasonable parent would consent to medical or surgical treatment, that is the test to apply notwithstanding any religious objections. If parents do not reasonably consent to treatment, the Local Authority Social Services department may then intervene and ultimately take the child into care.

Much of what we said earlier about the *Gillick* case could be repeated here. Mrs Gillick seemed to be arguing that a minor under the age of 16 is not capable of authorising any kind of medical treatment to his or her own body. But Lord Fraser said this was 'verging on the absurd': provided the patient was capable of understanding what was proposed and expressing his or her wishes, Lord Fraser said, he or she could consent to medical treatment.

## Social rights of children

At the age of 6 weeks a child can legally be handed over to prospective adoptive parents, though in practice they may not have to wait that long. There must be no financial payment by the new parents, otherwise a criminal offence is committed under the Adoption Act. It is not until the age of 4½ months that the child can be adopted.

As far as education is concerned, from the age of 2 the child can attend a nursery school and from the age of 5 it must undergo full-time education. At the age of 16 the child may leave school.

A child can drink alcohol in private from the age of 5 and can go into a bar with an adult, provided he does not consume alcohol, from the age of 14. At 16, he can drink cider, beer, porter, or perry with a meal in a pub but not at the bar. It is not until 18 that he can buy drinks in the bar of a pub, and not until the age of 21 that he can apply for a liquor licence.

## Financial rights of children

An account at a building society or bank (including the National Savings Bank) can be opened in a child's name from birth. Similarly the child may own premium bonds from that time. When the child is 7 he can pay into and draw money from a National Savings Bank or Trustee Savings Bank account. At the age of 13, a child may open a current account at a clearing bank so long as the bank manager agrees. People under 18 are not given cheque cards or credit cards.

On public transport, children under the age of 5 travel free. At 14 they have to pay full fare on British Rail; and at 16 full fare on buses and on the London Underground.

Supplementary benefit can be applied for by a child in his own right from the age of 16, but sickness and unemployment benefit are not available until 16½.

## Young criminals

A child cannot be convicted of a crime under the age of 10. From that age children may only be convicted if it can be shown that they knew that what they were doing was wrong. Their fingerprints may be taken with the consent of a parent or guardian.

At the age of 14 they can be convicted just like an adult and can be fined up to £400 or sent to a detention centre. Their fingerprints may be taken if they and a parent or guardian both agree.

At 15 a child may be sentenced to youth custody (which has replaced borstal and imprisonment for people under 21). At 17 a child may be tried on any charge in any court. At 21 he or she may be sent to prison (although some people under 21 sentenced to youth custody serve their time in adult prisons).

It is not, however, until the age of 18 that an individual becomes eligible to sit on a jury trying criminal cases in the Crown Court.

## Your rights as you grow up

There are many age limits governing the social behaviour of children and young adults. Among these are:

*Age 14:* A child can own an airgun.

*Age 15:* A child may own a shotgun and ammunition (providing the appropriate licence is obtained).

*Age 16:* A child may marry as long as there is parental agreement.

He may join a trade union.

He may choose his own doctor and agree to medical treatment on his own behalf.

He may buy fireworks.

He may buy cigarettes. (There is no minimum age for smoking cigarettes.)

He may drive a moped or a tractor.

A girl may consent to sexual intercourse.

A boy may join the armed services, so long as his parents agree.

*Age 17:* The child may use an airgun in a public place.

He may drive a motorcycle or a car.

He may go into a betting shop, but may not place a bet.

A girl may join the armed services if her parents agree.

At the age of 18, the child reaches the age of majority and assumes nearly all the rights and responsibilities of an adult. He may, for example, make a will, join the services without his parents' agreement, be tattooed, bet in a betting shop, own land, be eligible for jury service, marry without his parents' agreement, vote in elections provided he is on the electoral register, apply for a passport, become a blood donor and enter into binding agreements.

The age of majority used to be 21, and you still have to wait until you reach that age before standing as a candidate in an election, driving a bus and, if you're a man, consenting to homosexual acts in private.

## Can a child sue?

Everyone has the right to sue someone when their rights have been infringed. But a child (under 18) cannot sue in his own name. The parent (or guardian or other close relative) brings the action on behalf of the child and is known as the 'next friend'. In such cases a solicitor should be employed to ensure that the best interests of the child are secured in any negotiation or settlement of the claim.

So if, for example, a child is injured in a road accident, he has an equal right to recover damages for injuries received as an adult similarly injured, the only difference being that he sues through his 'next friend'.

## Rights and responsibilities

It is clear that children's rights increase from their birth until adulthood and beyond – as do their obligations. Here, the balance between rights and duties is perhaps most dramatically seen. Growing up implies assuming responsibilities, but with them comes the freedom to live within the law. There are, of course, implications for children in the criminal law and also within the family where there is a divorce or separation. These matters are dealt with in other parts of the book.

157

## Illegitimacy

When a child is born, the fact of its birth must be registered within six weeks at the district registry for births, marriages and death.

When this is done, a birth certificate is issued, which can be of two varieties. The first is a short form which does not give full details of the parents, thus not revealing whether a child is legitimate. The long form does give details of parents. Both forms are equally valid.

Illegitimacy means that a child is born to parents who are not married. A child is usually registered under its father's name, but where the mother and father are not married it can only be so registered at the joint request of both mother and father; or at the request of the mother only if she can produce a statutory declaration by a man admitting he's the father. The birth can also be registered in the father's name if there is already an order of the court (an affiliation order) stating that he is the father.

If a child is illegitimate the father has no right to request the child's registration in his name without the consent of the mother.

So, if a child is illegitimate the mother has sole parental rights and duties. Even if a father is paying maintenance towards the upbringing of a child, he has no say in what should happen to that child.

## Adoption

If a child is adopted there is a special form of registration called the Adopted Children's Register which will give the child a new birth certificate showing his adoptive parents together with the court that made the adoption order.

If a short form of birth certificate is issued, it will not show the fact that the child is adopted and this remains confidential information which is not available for public inspection.

## Surrogacy

Early in 1985 there was a great deal of interest in the activities of surrogate mothers. A lady called Kim Cotton had been artificially inseminated with a view to handing over her child, immediately after it was born, to its father and his wife. The story had a comparatively happy outcome thanks to the good sense of the father's lawyers and the High Court Family Division, but there was much concern that people like Mrs Cotton were being paid for the hire of their wombs.

The government's reaction was to rush through Parliament a bill designed to put commercial surrogate mother agencies out of business in Britain. Once Mrs Cotton had disappeared from the headlines the bill attracted surprisingly little attention and the Surrogacy Arrangements Act became law in the summer of 1985. It's not a particularly elegant piece of legislation, grappling with such unfamiliar concepts as 'embryo insertion' and taking seventeen lines to define a 'surrogacy arrangement' as an arrangement for a woman to carry a child with a view to it being handed over to someone who will then exercise parental rights over it. No attempt, incidentally, is made to say what 'parental rights' are.

The Act creates a number of new criminal offences for which the maximum penalty is three months in prison. These all relate to making surrogacy arrangements in exchange for money. The would-be mother is not breaking the law by her involvement in the deal; nor is the child's father; nor, it seems, is anyone else for whom the surrogate mother is carrying the child (such as the father's wife).

Since it's assumed that surrogacy agencies can't work unless they can advertise for customers, the Act makes it illegal to publish advertisements by would-be surrogate mothers, and people (including agencies) who want to find them. The maximum penalty is a fine of £2,000.

The parliamentary draftsman may well have thought he was treading on dangerous ground in this hitherto virgin territory; to avoid unwanted prosecutions he has inserted a section requiring the consent of the Director of Public Prosecutions before proceedings can be brought. The Act was passed before the Crown Prosecution Service began taking many of the prosecution decisions that previously had to be made by the Director himself.

## Changing your name

We are all given names at birth and take the surname of our parents. What are your rights if you wish to change your name? In general, an adult can call himself or herself by any name they want to. But think of the confusion that could be caused if your real name is Black and you choose to call yourself White. Imagine the suspicion that this could cause with official bodies.

The simple fact is that organisations like the Inland Revenue or the Department of Health and Social Security will not like it very much unless you can prove that your adoption of another name is not for fraudulent purposes. So the sensible thing to do, if you are bent on changing your name, is to confirm the position in any one of three ways.

First, and the most official, is to change your name by deed poll. To do this, you really need to go to a solicitor who will prepare a formal 'deed' (or statement of intention to change a name) which has to be signed in your old and your new name in front of a witness. That deed is then stamped by the Inland Revenue and a small fee is payable. This document can then be lodged at the Supreme Court as definitive evidence of the change of name – though this bit isn't normally essential. The whole exercise is unlikely to cost more than £20.

Secondly you can make what is called a statutory declaration, which is a sworn statement declaring the change of name. Again you need to use a solicitor and it is unlikely to cost you more than £15 or 20.

Thirdly, and perhaps least satisfactory for official purposes, would be a letter from a person of standing in the local community (such as a doctor, priest, or a magistrate) stating that your new name is the one by which you are commonly known. This, though, is unlikely to satisfy the taxman or your bank and the best advice would be to get one of the more official-looking documents as proof that you really have changed your name.

Do not forget, though, that you can never change the name on your birth certificate.

# 5 Housing

The law relating to the ownership of land and buildings which stand on it is one of the most ancient areas of the English legal system. The land has always been closely related to the economy of the country; and in feudal times, when agriculture was dominant, the ownership of the ground and the crops which it produced formed the basis of society. Much of our modern law exists on the basis of those feudal times, and the law developed over the centuries until a great turning-point in land law occurred in 1925. The statutes passed in the 1920s form the basis of modern law relating to the ownership of land and property and the rights and duties arising from it. This is an area of the law which is very complicated, and this chapter will only provide an outline of what is one of the most technical concepts in our law.

We all have to live somewhere. It may be in a house or a flat, we may own it or we may be a tenant. Rights concerning land and property are unique. The land will never wear out and never needs to be replaced. It is something which lasts forever, so its ownership is crucial and therefore subject to particular procedures and terminology.

There are two basic ways of having an interest in land – as either a freeholder or a leaseholder. A freeholder owns the land and what stands on it for ever; he can do more or less what he likes with it. A leaseholder owns the land for a fixed period of time only. It follows that every piece of land has a freeholder, but if a lease has been granted on that land then the leaseholder owes certain duties to the freeholder. The freeholder also owes certain duties to the leaseholder, of course.

## THE RIGHT TO LAND

What then are our rights relating to our interest in land and property? We have seen that a freeholder owns the land forever, but this in modern times is always subject to certain restrictions – for example gas and electricity authorities will have certain rights and duties over his land. A long leasehold in many ways confers similar rights to the leaseholder except he will have to pay ground rent to the freeholder and when the lease expires, the land will revert to the freeholder.

### Tenant's rights

If you rent your house or flat, the law which deals with your rights is very complicated. It is set out in the Rent Acts and whole books have been written on them. There are more than a dozen different types of tenancy, but the basic rule is that most people who rent homes from a private landlord fall within the Rent Acts.

To complicate matters further, even if the Rent Acts apply they may give either full or restricted protection to the tenant. Basically, if the tenancy began after 14 August 1974 the tenant is protected unless the landlord is also resident on the premises. He doesn't have to live with the tenant; he is still considered to be resident even if he has a separate flat in the same building.

We all hear stories about people being evicted from their homes, but the state of the law at present is quite clear: nobody can be evicted from their home except with an order from the court. The court will not make an order unless the tenant has broken part of his contract – if, for example, he has not paid the rent, or his tenancy has expired. The landlord has to be careful to ensure that he is behaving reasonably as the criminal law makes harassment of a tenant a criminal offence. Therefore a tenant has a right to be protected from a landlord who, for example, locks him out, makes the building unsafe, or continually insults him.

A tenant also has a right to know where he stands. A landlord must provide a weekly tenant with a rent book; the tenant has the right to know the name and address of his landlord; and any service charge (such as for maintenance, insurance or administration) must be reasonable. Landlords must consult tenants before incurring expenditure over a certain value and obtain estimates for the cost of the work to be done.

The law on repairing and maintaining privately rented property is complex in the extreme. Generally the landlord is responsible for repairs to the structure of the property, but it will depend on the length of the lease which the tenant holds.

All leases are different and tenants may well, as part of their leases, undertake to do or not do certain things (for example, not to play loud music late at night).

As we've said, a book like this cannot possibly deal comprehensively with landlord and tenant matters, but one thing is for sure – if you think that you have a landlord and tenant problem you will certainly need legal advice. The best place to find a solicitor if you don't already have one, or if a friend can't recommend one, is by going to your local library or Citizens Advice Bureau and asking for the Solicitors Regional Directory which lists all solicitors in your area and gives an indication of the types of work which they specialise in.

## Buying a house or flat

Let's look briefly at the process of buying and selling land – conveyancing. Because the law relating to land is so ancient and complicated, certain 'searches' have to be carried out to ensure that you are getting what you think you are. For example, it is important to know whether somebody else has a right over your land or whether there are plans to build a motorway over it or an airport on it.

Searches conducted by you or your solicitor before you sign the contract will reveal any problems and ensure that you don't end up buying a liability. A house or flat is, after all, the most expensive and important item that most people ever buy, so it's important to make sure that it is problem-free. Because these procedures are so crucial, only solicitors have been allowed to do conveyancing work for money up to now. Their comprehensive legal training is designed to alert them to any problems concerning the land you want to buy, and they can give you independent advice about how to cope with them.

However, in recent years there has been pressure to open up this area of legal work to non-solicitors. In 1984 the government set up a committee chaired by Professor Julian Farrand to examine the possibilities of extending the right to do conveyancing to non-solicitors, and to establish what qualifications should be required of any new body of conveyancers.

Professor Farrand's report recommended the setting up of a body of 'licensed conveyancers' who need not be solicitors but would be governed by a professional 'council' and subject to certain educational and ethical standards. That report was accepted by the government and the Administration of Justice Act 1985 provides for the setting up of a Council for Licensed Conveyancers and gives that body authority to make suitable rules and regulations.

So during the next few years, as the Council for Licensed Conveyancers gets under way and sets the standards and rules, a new body of conveyancers will emerge within the legal world.

You will then have the right either to go to a solicitor (with his wider knowledge of the law) or to a licensed conveyancer (who may have other advantages) when you wish to buy or sell land and property. Or of course you can do the job yourself, if you're up to it. You'll save solicitors' fees (which are pretty low these days) but you will still have to pay stamp duty (if it applies) and the other legal fees (and agent's charges) which a solicitor or convenyancer has to pass on to you. It will take up a lot of your time and there's nobody to sue if it goes wrong. But even saving £100 by doing the job yourself can give you a great deal of satisfaction.

## The people next door

Wherever you live, there will be someone next door, and of course you have rights and duties in relation to them. You have the right not to be pestered or inconvenienced by them and they have the right not to be pestered or inconvenienced by you.

Everyone is familiar with the notice which states 'Trespassers will be prosecuted'. In fact this is completely wrong, as trespass is generally a civil matter not a criminal offence, and it is not normally possible to prosecute anyone for trespassing. However, if anyone enters your property without your invitation or authority you have the right to ask him to leave or if necessary eject him. The rule is that if you have to eject the trespasser (because he won't leave when you ask him to), you must not use any more force than is reasonable to enforce your rights. You are not, therefore, entitled to fire a shotgun at an old lady who has strayed onto your land during a country stroll.

It may be that there is a right of way or a public footpath passing over your land. If this is so, then people are entitled to cross your land, provided it is in the course of a proper journey. You cannot, for example, park your caravan on a public right of way and stay there for three weeks.

Trespass is therefore the actual presence of a person on your land when he is not entitled to be there. There may be other ways in which neighbours and other people can invade your privacy by making a nuisance of themselves. This might be by playing loud music at three o'clock in the morning or by experimenting with chemicals to make an unpleasant smell which wafts into your dining room at lunchtime.

If you wish to bring an action for nuisance in the courts (and most lawyers will advise you not to, unless the nuisance is intolerable, because it is much better to resolve these matters amicably without going to court), then once again the test which will be applied is one of reasonableness. This will be affected by the nature of the interference, the nature of the premises and the surroundings, and how it interferes with your quality of life.

So what is nuisance in one area may not be considered a nuisance in another – if you live next door to the brickworks or a sewage farm, no court is likely to uphold an action for nuisance because of the smell!

## When you have visitors

Everybody who comes to your house as a visitor is owed a series of duties by you. If Aunt Maud comes to lunch and the ceiling falls in and hits her on the head, then you, the occupier, are liable, provided it can be shown that you were negligent – that you knew that the ceiling was likely to fall down and had done nothing about it. Again it will all depend on the circumstances of the accident and the people involved. An occupier cannot be responsible if a child has wandered onto his land and because of childish curiosity has put himself in danger. But a landowner does have a duty to make his land reasonably childproof if there are risks and dangers there.

If you have the builders in to do work in your house and somebody is injured because of the builders' negligence, then they, not you, will be liable.

## Your animals

What about the dog or the cat (at which you may already have thrown this book after reading page 21)?

If household pets stray and cause damage to neighbours or their property, again the question of whether the pet owner has been negligent is relevant. What is reasonable? If your dog runs into the street and causes an accident and it can be shown that you were negligent in allowing the animal to stray, then you may well be liable. If you keep dangerous animals, then you will be liable for injury or damage even if you were not negligent.

Similarly if you keep livestock (such as cows, horses, goats, pigs and sheep) then special provisions apply and you are liable for damage caused whether you were negligent or not.

All of this sounds as if it is about duties rather than rights, but don't forget that if you were on the receiving end of any of these problems then you would have the right to enforce your neighbour's duty to you.

# Rights of entry

We are all familiar with the maxim that an Englishman's home is his castle. That phrase arose from the writings of Sir Edward Coke who died in 1634, and most people are jealous of the principle that their own home is their escape from the cares of the world. The front door is closed at night and the rest of life can be forgotten until the next day. But is that really so? The answer is clearly no. But how many people know the extent to which statutory bodies and the like can send along their representatives to your home and force their way in if necessary?

## Public utilities

Let's take the obvious ones first. We all use public service amenities – gas, electricity, water – and they are all provided by the relevant authority. The gas man and the electricity man call to read the meter and we think no more of it. But what are the powers of those authorities to enter into our homes?

The electricity board and the gas board have the right to enter any premises to which electricity or gas has been supplied. The relevant board must first obtain the consent of the occupier of the premises; and if that is not possible or is refused, he may apply to a magistrate for a warrant. In order to obtain this he must swear in writing that entry to the premises is reasonably required for a particular purpose.

The magistrate must be satisfied that entry to the premises was only sought after 24 hours notice of intended entry had been given to the occupier; or that entry was required in a case of emergency and was refused; or that the premises were unoccupied.

An emergency arises in a case where the official has reasonable cause to believe that circumstances exist which are likely to endanger life or property and that immediate entry onto the property is necessary to verify the existence of such circumstances and to put things right as necessary.

If a warrant is allowed by the magistrate, then it remains in force until the purpose for which entry was required is accomplished. If the official enters premises which are unoccupied or if the occupier is away, then he has a duty to leave the place as secure against trespassers as it was when he arrived.

The water board too have powers to enter your home. They must give 24 hours notice to the occupier of the premises and they may obtain a warrant if permission is refused. Obstructing a relevant official may lead to prosecution and, on conviction, a fine. In addition, if the water board have reason to suspect that there is waste or misuse of water they are empowered to enter premises. Refusal may again result in prosecution.

A water board official may also, on production of suitable identification, enter premises to inspect any water meters, or ascertain whether there has been any contravention of regulations relating to water, to see if there are circumstances requiring the water board to carry out any work or for the purpose of doing any such work. Once again, 24 hours notice must be given, or a warrant obtained from a magistrate, and any obstruction of the official can result in prosecution which, if successful, can lead to a fine.

## Tax officials

What about the taxman? Anyone who is required to make a tax return and who fails to do so can be required by the Inland Revenue to deliver accounts or to make them available for inspection. The taxman is then entitled to take copies of or extracts from anything which he has seen.

If you own land or other assets which the Inland Revenue need to value for the purpose of calculating how much tax is to be paid, the taxman (who must be able to prove his entitlement to do so) can, at any reasonable time, enter the land to assess its value for capital gains tax or capital transfer tax. Similarly, if the Revenue need to determine the market value of an object which you own, then you are obliged to let the taxman see it for valuation at any reasonable time.

If you intentionally delay or obstruct the carrying out of such

168

valuations, you run the risk of a criminal prosecution. Obstructing the taxman does not necessarily mean the use of physical violence towards him – the courts have decided that anything which you do to make it more difficult for the official to carry out his duty can amount to obstruction.

The Customs and Excise also have powers of entry both in connection with the collection of Value Added Tax and with the paying of Customs Duty on goods.

Let's take the VATman first. The Finance Act of 1972 sets up the VAT authority in this country and, in order to exercise any of its powers, an authorised official of the Customs and Excise may at any reasonable time enter premises used for carrying out a business. Obviously this may include your home. If the VATman has cause to believe that your premises are being used for the supply of goods which are subject to VAT, then he may enter and inspect the building and the goods.

If the VATman believes that an offence is being committed in connection with the payment of the tax, then he can go before a Justice of the Peace and, on oath, set out his suspicions. If the magistrate is satisfied that there are reasonable grounds for believing him, then a warrant will be issued allowing the premises to be entered, if necessary by force, at any time within the following fourteen days.

When the warrant is executed, the official is entitled to remove anything whatsoever from the premises which he believes may provide evidence. He is also entitled to search anyone on the premises who he thinks might have committed an offence or be in possession of any relevant documents.

The Customs and Excise are also responsible for the collection of duties payable on certain commodities. We have all seen the customs men on our way back from holiday checking to make sure we are not over the duty-free limits, but they are also responsible for goods which are imported as cargo on ships or aeroplanes or are being stored in warehouses.

Powers of entry into premises are fairly wide. If a customs official believes that any article on which duty should have been paid is being kept in any building, then provided he has obtained a warrant from a magistrate, he can enter at any time during the day or night, to search for and confiscate such articles. Night means the hours between 11 pm and 5 am and entry during that time has to be in the company of a policeman. In order to gain entry, he is specifically authorised to break open any door, window or container and may force or remove any other obstruction.

If you are a tenant, whether of a private landlord or a local authority, the landlord has certain powers to enter your home.

## Council officials

A local authority acting as a landlord has certain obligations imposed on it concerning maintenance of the property. If the house needs repairs, then the local authority must carry them out, and when they are about to do so they must serve notice on the occupier who, if he obstructs them, may be liable to prosecution.

If works have been carried out on a local authority property, then the relevant official, after giving 24 hours written notice to the occupier of the house, may enter in order to find out whether the work has been properly done.

If the local authority has reason to believe that housing regulations have been contravened or that it is necessary to exercise other powers under the Housing Acts, it may get a warrant from a magistrate allowing entry into the house. If, when the official goes into the premises (whether or not by force) the occupier is not there, then there is a duty on him to leave the house as secure against trespassers as he found it.

In some inner-city areas there may be houses which still do not have the standard amenities. In such cases the tenant has certain rights to have them installed. The local authority again has the right to enter in order to survey what needs to be done and in order to instal the necessary facilities.

There are also powers under the Public Health Act for council officials to enter houses where it is thought that there might be breaches of public health regulations or bye-laws. They must give 24 hours notice and if admission is refused or if the case is urgent, then they can again apply to the court for a warrant.

If a compulsory purchase order is being considered, the relevant authority is entitled to enter the land in order to value it, so long as he has given 24 hours notice of his intention to the occupier. Again obstruction of the official could lead to a prosecution.

## Other intruders

Those then are the main bodies who have rights of entry into your home. But there are some rather more obscure circumstances where you could find your carpet being trampled over by the bureaucrats. Let's look at some of them.

If you are a farmer, or indeed employ anyone in an agricultural capacity, you must comply with the provisions of the Agricultural Wages Act. Among these are requirements to keep wage sheets and records relating to your employees. Once again, officials can at all times enter your home, provided they have given you reasonable notice, and inspect your records.

If you are a radio ham, you have to have a licence under the Wireless Telegraphy Act to transmit your messages. That licence may include a provision allowing a right of entry into your home.

Fire inspectors and firemen also have authority to enter. The Fire inspector has to give you 24 hours notice, but if you don't let the fire brigade in, you could be liable to a fine.

And, finally, the Food Act of 1984, the Poultry Meat (Hygiene) Regulations 1976, and the Fresh Meat Export (Hygiene and Inspection) Regulations 1981 all give powers for officials to enter your home as long as the standard 24 hours notice has been given to you.

So, although you do have rights of privacy in your home and rights to occupy it as you wish, there are circumstances where officials have the authority to override those rights.

This is an extension of the principle that for every right there is a balancing duty or obligation. The equation here is that a person has a right to the supply of certain essential services, but the obligation resulting from that right is allowing the relevant official to check, maintain, and prevent abuse of that supply.

# 6 The law and the consumer

We are all consumers in one sense of the word or another. We all buy goods – such as food, clothes, furniture and luxuries. Some of us may sell things to other people. In our society we earn money in order to be able to exchange that money for goods or services.

## SALE OF GOODS

What are your rights when you buy something? Well, the law has been concerned with the relationship between buyer and seller for a very long time. The first Sale of Goods Act was passed by Parliament in 1893 and there has been constant legislation to give the consumer more protection as the years have progressed.

Whenever you go into a shop to buy something, you make a contract with the seller. People selling things are responsible in law for the quality and fitness of the things they offer to the public. The modern law is set out in the Sale of Goods Act 1979. That Act implies three promises in the contract made by the seller to the customer. They are:

* that the goods are as described;
* that they are fit for the use for which they were intended; and
* that they are of suitable merchantable quality.

In addition, the Misrepresentation Act 1967 provides that a seller must not tell lies about the goods on offer when persuading the customer to buy them.

Let's look at each of these in turn. First, the shopkeeper must ensure that the goods he sells are as described by him. This simply means that items for sale must be what they say they are. For example, if a jersey is labelled as 'pure wool', that is exactly what it must be, not 50% wool and 50% nylon.

Secondly, goods must be fit for the purpose for which they

were intended. For example, if you buy a fountain pen to write to your Aunt Maud in Australia, you assume that when you fill it with ink you will be able to write with it. If it does not work, then it is not fit for the purpose for which it was intended and the shopkeeper who sold it to you is in breach of the contract you made with him when you bought it.

Thirdly, when you buy goods they must be of suitable merchantable quality. This is something which is not so easy to define. You have to bear in mind the price at which the item was sold and the way in which it was described. If goods are second-hand, then obviously you would expect a lower quality than if they were brand new. Problems can arise when considering how long something should reasonably be expected to last and function properly. If you buy a radio for £150 you would normally expect it to last longer than one which only cost £5.

The test here, as in so many areas of the law, is what can reasonably be expected bearing in mind all the circumstances of the case. If you buy a pair of jeans and the zip goes within two weeks, then you would be entitled to return them to the shop. If the zip didn't go until you had had the jeans for 2 years, then it would not be reasonable to return them.

The fourth point, that the seller must tell the truth about the goods, means that any statement of fact made about an item must be true. So if you buy a clock and the seller tells you that it chimes on the hour, and it does not, then he will have misrepresented the goods to you and be in breach of contract.

All this then gives you certain rights in respect of things which you buy. They are rights to enable you to get what you pay for. What does the law allow you to do to enforce those rights? Well, if you have goods which you are dissatisfied with for reasons described above, the first thing to do is to take them back to the shop where you bought them and complain. If you are justified in your complaint then you are entitled to have your money back provided you act quickly. If you wait too long you may be deemed to have 'accepted' the goods and you may only get damages. (You can, of course, have the goods replaced, but only if the shopkeeper agrees.)

Sometimes shopkeepers will offer you a 'credit note', but again – if you are justified in your complaint – you do not have to accept this as your remedy. Similarly, you do not have to agree to send the goods back to the manufacturer. The contract of sale was made with the shop, not the manufacturer, and you are entitled to your money back from the shop.

## Supply of services

This then is all to do with buying goods; but you also spend money and enter into contracts with people who provide services, whether they are painting your house or repairing your washing machine. Different rules apply here, but their intention is the same: that the consumer should have a proper job done for the money he is paying.

The rules here are:

* that the work will be done as agreed between you and the contractor;
* that any parts or materials used will be of proper quality;
* that reasonable care will be taken of property belonging to you; and
* that the work will be done to a reasonable standard.

Let's look at each of these rules in turn.

First, that the work will be done as agreed. This means that the customer is only liable for work which he has authorised. For example, if you take your bicycle to the repair shop to have a puncture mended and when you collect it the shop has also installed a completely new gear system, then you will not be liable to pay for the gear system – as you had not asked for that work to be done. This is where it becomes so important to be clear about what you have asked for; and why it is always sensible to put things in writing. If you do not, the chances are that the bicycle repairer would say that you had asked for the gear system to be installed and it becomes your word against his. So, make it easy for your rights to be enforced and put things in writing (keeping copies, of course.)

Secondly, parts or materials must be of proper quality and fit for the purpose for which they were intended. This is similar to the shopkeeper's duty, as here the supplier of the services is also supplying goods.

Thirdly, proper care must be taken of your property. If you entrust your goods to someone else, they must take reasonable steps to look after them. For example, if you take your watch into a jewellers to get a new strap and find when you collect it that the glass is broken because someone in the shop has dropped it, then the jeweller has not taken reasonable care of your watch and must compensate you for it.

Finally, work must be done to a reasonable standard. Anyone who offers a service, or a skill, must be able to perform that service to a reasonable standard of competence. The problem is: what is reasonable? This will depend to a large extent on who is doing the job. If your washing machine goes wrong and you call in a fully qualified plumber who has served a proper apprenticeship and works full time on plumbing, you can expect a higher standard than if you call in an odd job man who happened to fix somebody else's washing machine two years ago but has not touched one since. Again, what has to be proved is what is a reasonable standard of workmanship in all the circumstances.

## Your rights and your remedies

What do you do if one of these things goes wrong? Well, what you want is the defective work to be put right; and most reasonable tradesmen, if you complain and they accept that complaint is justified, will make good the defects. If you can't agree or there is a dispute, then remedy will be to sue the contractor in the courts (see Chapter 2).

These then are the rights given to you as a consumer and the duties imposed on people selling goods or services. What happens, though, if you buy something on hire purchase or buy something on credit? In our current times of inflation, credit sales have become increasingly popular as they allow the consumer to obtain the goods immediately and pay for them later or after an agreed period of time. As this popularity has grown, so the law has had to develop with it.

Let's look at hire purchase first. This means exactly what it says. When the agreement is initially made, an arrangement is made with a finance company for the purchase price to be paid by way of instalments. What happens effectively is that the shop sells the item to the finance company who then hires it to you until the final instalment is paid, when it becomes yours. So, until the payments are completed, you do not own the goods.

If goods are bought by credit sale (this is not the same as by credit card, which we'll come to later), then the purchaser becomes the owner of the goods at once. The shop sells them to the finance company which sells them on to you and you pay the finance company back in instalments. The crucial difference therefore between a hire purchase transaction and a credit sale is that because you are the owner immediately in a credit sale, then you can re-sell the goods before the loan is paid off. With a hire purchase agreement, the fact that you do not become the owner until the last instalment is paid means that you cannot sell the goods involved until that time.

Credit cards are now widely used by most of us. We are all familiar with how they work. The shopkeeper invoices the credit card company for the cost of the items bought and you pay the credit card company later when they invoice you.

If you buy goods or services worth more than £100 with a credit card and they are faulty in some respect, your rights are not diminished. The Consumer Credit Act 1974 gives you as the consumer equal rights against the credit card company and the shopkeeper who sold you the goods. The company and the shopkeeper become jointly liable to you. This can be advantageous if, for example, the shop where you bought the goods has gone bust; in such a case you would still be able to claim your money back from the credit card company, so you are in fact better off than if you had made a cash purchase. This only applies to credit cards (such as Barclaycard and Access); not charge cards such as American Express or Diner's Club. You may only have limited protection if your card was first issued before July 1977, but don't be put off trying, as the card companies may still meet your claim.

Apart from the civil law of breach of contract, the criminal law has developed to protect the consumer. For example, the Trade Descriptions Act makes it a criminal offence for traders to describe goods or services falsely. The Trading Standards Office in each local area can prosecute traders who are guilty of an offence and it is often a good idea if you have suffered from false or misleading statements to report the shop to the Trading Standards Office, whose telephone number will be in your local directory, under the name of your local council. If the Trading Standards Officer brings a prosecution, the court may order the trader to pay you compensation.

If you are buying food, then there are very strict regulations under the Food and Drugs Act imposed on the seller. Food must be fit for human consumption and if you feel that food you have bought is not of proper quality, or that a food shop is unhygienic, you should complain to the environmental health officer who has the power to prosecute.

It is also a criminal offence if you are 'sold short'. For example, if you ask for a pound of potatoes you must get a pound and not 15 ounces. The Weights and Measures Act 1963 gives the local Weights and Measures department power to prosecute shopkeepers; so if you feel that you have been given short measure, then complain to them.

The Trade Descriptions Act also imposes criminal liability on shopkeepers who mislead customers by the information given on price labels. For example, it is a criminal offence to offer a watch for sale with a label showing the price of £50 deleted and £20 substituted unless the watch was at one time sold at the higher price. Similarly, prices displayed on goods in a shop window must be the same as the prices on the same goods inside the shop.

These then are your most important rights as a consumer – rights which you should know and be familiar with. It is always slightly daunting to complain: no one likes to make a fuss, and people are often reluctant to return goods to shops because they are not really sure what their rights are. Shopkeepers can be very

177

intimidating and the courage of your convictions can easily be lost. Don't be afraid to enforce your rights – you know what they are now and that's why they're there.

## HOLIDAYS

Has that time of year come around again when you are thinking about where to go on holiday? Most of us will take a trip down to the local travel agent's office and browse through the many holiday brochures which will be on display there.

We all know what holiday brochures are like – those glossy pages and promises of the most marvellous time of your life, descriptions of the facilities available at each hotel or resort, glowing references to long sandy beaches and the like. Undoubtedly the brochures are designed to persuade you to go to a particular place; but what happens if, when you arrive, it is a very different story from what you have been led to believe? What happens if there is no swimming pool at the hotel when you have specifically been promised one? At worst, what happens if the hotel has not even been built? We have all heard horror stories about holidays which, after all, are something which people spend many months saving for and looking forward to. So what are your rights? Let's first take a look at the structure of the holiday industry.

### Your rights as a holiday maker

A package holiday (which is after all what most of us buy) is exactly that. It is a package including flights, transport from the airport to the hotel, accommodation, meals and any other items offered on your particular holiday. Packages are normally put together by tour operators, and it is the tour operators with whom you enter into the contract for the holiday. Most holidays are sold through travel agents and they are agents for the tour operator. They are, if you like, the salesmen of the industry. The travel agent does not arrange the details of the package holiday; he is only concerned with the selling of the package to you, the customer, and possibly with selling other items such as train tickets and plane tickets which do not form part of a package.

Let's now look at the holiday brochure. It is here that any suggestions of false or misleading statements are likely to arise. Most complaints relate to statements made in the brochure about the facilities available at the particular hotel or resort. Statements in holiday brochures are representations designed to induce the customer to enter into a contract for a particular holiday package. A representation must be a statement of fact (as distinct from a statement of opinion), and where a tour operator has clearly made a misrepresentation, then he will be liable both under criminal and civil law.

## Complaining to the local council

The Trade Descriptions Act 1968 provides that anyone who in the course of his trade or business makes a statement which he knows to be false, concerning the nature of any services or facilities to be provided by him, will be guilty of an offence. As we've said, that part of the Act is enforced by the Trading Standards Department of Local Authorities. Every area has a Local Trading Standards office and any prosecutions brought under the Act have to be reported to the Office of Fair Trading. A prosecution as outlined above does not, of course, prevent the dissatisfied individual from pursuing the matter through the civil courts and seeking financial compensation through that route. He may get compensation anyway as the result of a prosecution.

## Complaining through the courts

The Misrepresentation Act of 1967 provides that where a person has entered into a contract relying on a statement made to him by the other party to the contract (whether orally or in writing or in this case in the holiday brochure), and that statement turns out to be false, then the person complaining is entitled to cancel the contract and may be awarded damages by the court.

If the dissatisfied consumer decides to pursue the matter through the courts, then there may be several options open to him. It is likely that the claim will fall within the jurisdiction of the county court as very few holidays cost more than £5,000, which is the county court limit. So a normal county court civil action will have to be launched just as we described in Chapter 2, which deals with the courts and their procedures. Your claim might be more than £5,000 if you have suffered further losses as a consequence of the misrepresentation.

If, however, you are not claiming more than £500 then you can use the less formal procedure for small claims in the county court which, as we've said, will not normally require the expense of instructing lawyers to represent the parties.

## Complaining to an arbitrator

There is a third option for the consumer. The Association of British Travel Agents have a conciliation and arbitration scheme which has been running since 1975. The basic principle of this scheme is that tour operators should wherever possible take all practical steps to resolve complaints from dissatisfied customers. If a complaint cannot be resolved sensibly, then the customer can contact the Association of British Travel Agents for help. A conciliation officer may then be appointed to intervene in the dispute and see if he can resolve matters between the parties. If he cannot sort things out, then the consumer is entitled to make a formal application to the Chartered Institute of Arbitrators for the matter to be settled by arbitration (which we described on page 54). In such a case, the tour operator must consent to the arbitration and agree to be bound by it. Any application for arbitration must be made within 9 months of the end of the holiday and the holidaymaker too must agree to be bound by the decision of the arbitrator. There will not be an oral hearing: the abitrator will come to his decision based on documentary evidence provided to him by the parties.

Do not forget that the tour operator's brochure which you pick up in the travel agent's shop, as well as showing you what holidays are available, is also an advertisement for the tour operator concerned, designed to promote his business. That means that the code of practice of the self-appointed Advertising Standards Authority will apply to it. If a complaint is made to them about a particular brochure, the Authority will investigate the complaint and decide whether or not it is valid. Adverse publicity for the tour operator if a complaint is upheld could be very damaging indeed to his reputation. No one after all is going to want to put their holiday savings into the hands of a firm which has a track record of unreliability.

So you see that it is possible to get redress for a disastrous holiday and it does not necessarily mean incurring the expense, time and formality of going to court, as the various arbitration schemes show. You do have rights in this area of our activities but it is up to you to ensure that those rights are enforced.

# 7 Work

Most of us need to go to work in order to earn enough money to enable us to house ourselves, clothe ourselves and feed ourselves and our families. The majority of people are employed by another person or an organisation. You go to work for them and you are paid a wage or a salary in recognition of the service you give the organisation or the individual. What rights does an employee have? Employment legislation over the years has become increasingly more complex and there are many more regulations governing working life than ever before.

## WORKERS' RIGHTS

Let's start at the beginning. You go for a job interview and you are lucky enough to be offered a job. As soon as you have accepted that offer, a contract of employment exists between you and your employer and you are both bound by the terms offered and agreed. The law states that within 13 weeks of starting work your employer must give you a written statement containing certain 'terms of employment' together with an additional statement concerning disciplinary and grievance procedures. The statement must include the names of both the employer and employee, the date when the employment began, a statement of the pay to be received, the intervals at which pay is to be given, the hours which are to be worked, holiday entitlement, an outline of sickness payment, an outline of any pension scheme, a statement of the length of notice which the employee is obliged to give and entitled to receive, and the title of the job which the employee has been taken on to do.

This applies to all employees except those who work less than 16 hours a week (unless they have been employed for at least

8 hours a week for at least five years), certain merchant seamen and fishermen; crown servants; and registered dock workers engaged on dock work.

So you start your new job and you receive your statement of the terms of your employment. The first pay day is approaching and most people have a statutory right to receive a written statement of pay at the time of payment. An itemised pay statement must contain the gross amount of the wage or salary; the amounts of any deductions (such as for National Insurance); and the net amount of wage or salary payable. You will not be entitled to a pay statement if you ordinarily work outside Great Britain, if you are a member of a police force, a merchant seaman, a fisherman paid entirely by his share in the profits of a fishing vessel, or a person who works less than 16 hours a week (unless you have been employed continuously for at least 8 hours a week for at least five years).

## Entitlement to time off

Certain employees are entitled to time off in certain circumstances. Let's first look at the increasing number of women at work who are pregnant. An employee who is expecting a baby acquires certain rights in relation to her employment. They do not apply to members of a police force, or the armed services, or women who work outside Great Britain under the terms of their contract of employment. First, a pregnant woman has the right to time off work for antenatal care, and payment for any such absence. If an employer dismisses a pregnant woman because she is pregnant or for any other reason connected with her pregnancy, then she will have the right to complain of unfair dismissal (see page 185). The exception to this is in circumstances where the dismissal due to pregnancy arises where the condition of the woman makes it impossible for her to do her job properly or where it would be against the law for her to do a particular job while pregnant. In these cases the employer must first offer the woman a suitable alternative vacancy if one is available before dismissing her.

There are rights for women to receive maternity pay. The

entitlement arises for the first six weeks of absence due to pregnancy or confinement starting at or after the beginning of the 11th week before the expected birth of the child. Those six weeks pay do not have to be taken in one unbroken period. The maternity pay due for each week is nine-tenths of a normal week's pay, less National Insurance contributions and maternity allowance. To qualify for maternity pay the woman must have been employed continuously for at least two years before the beginning of the 11th week and must continue to be employed by her employer even if she is not at work until immediately before the beginning of the 11th week. There is an obligation on the woman to notify her employer that she intends to stop work due to pregnancy at least 21 days before she does so. If that is not reasonably practical or there is some crisis in the pregnancy, the woman must inform her employer as soon as reasonably possible, in which case the employer is entitled to ask for a doctor's or midwife's certificate.

A woman has the right to return to her former job at any time before the end of 29 weeks after her child is born. She is entitled to be employed on terms and conditions not less favourable than those on which she worked before. When maternity leave has started, the employer has the right to ask the employee to confirm in writing whether or not she intends to return to work. The employee must inform her employer in writing of the date she proposes to come back, at least 21 days before that date.

The law requires employers to allow employees who hold certain public positions sufficient time off to perform the duties associated with those positions. People who are covered by these provisions are magistrates; members of a local council; members of a regional or district health authority; members of a water authority; members of a governing body of a school or college; and members of any statutory tribunal. The employer must allow such a person to attend meetings of the particular body of which he is a member, or any of its committees or sub-committees, and to carry out duties approved by that body which are necessary for discharging its functions. There is no obligation for the employer to pay the employee for time off for these purposes; at the same time there is nothing to prevent an employer from so paying.

## Trade union rights

The law also gives employees certain rights in respect of trade unions. There is a right not to be dismissed for belonging to a trade union, and the right not to be chosen for redundancy by virtue of belonging to a trade union. Employees who are members of trade unions have rights relating to their union activities. There is a right not to be dismissed for taking part in trade union activities at an appropriate time (this is either outside working hours or within working hours where the employer has agreed that the employee may take part in such activities). The nature of trade union activities in which an employee may take part have not been set out in the law. But actions on behalf of the trade union, for example as a shop steward, would be covered; so would activities connected with the election of trade union officials. It is important to note that industrial action does not count as a trade union activity.

Where there is no closed shop agreement, employees have the right not to belong to a trade union. They may not be dismissed for not belonging to a union or for refusing to join one; they may not be compelled by their employer to become a trade union member; and they may not be made redundant because they are not trade union members. A closed shop agreement is an arrangement between an employer and one trade union, or possibly more, requiring certain categories of employee to be members of those unions.

## Unfair dismissal

The law sets out fairly detailed provisions relating to the unfair dismissal of employees. Dismissal is the termination of employment by the employer with or without notice; or by the employee's resignation with or without notice where the person has resigned because the employer has shown an intention to be in breach of the contract of employment. Most employees have the right to complain to an industrial tribunal in cases of unfair dismissal. Such a complaint must be made by the individual who was dismissed and it applies to all individuals except those who have not completed 24 months continuous employment with their employer at the date of termination; people who work less than 16 hours a week unless they have been employed continuously for 8 hours a week for at least 5 years; people who have reached the normal retiring age before their effective date of termination; people with fixed term contracts where the dismissal consists only of the expiry of contract without renewal and where the employee has previously agreed to forgo a right of complaint in such circumstances; members of a police force and the armed services; registered dock workers engaged on dock work; and certain people working on fishing boats who are paid solely by a share in the profits or gross earnings of the fishing vessel.

A dismissal can only be fair if the employer can show a reason for dismissal relating to:

* the employee's conduct;
* the employee's capability or qualification for the job;
* redundancy (where the employer's need for the employee's function has ended);

or if there is some other substantial reason justifying dismissal. An employee also has the right not to be dismissed on grounds of sexual or racial discrimination, as we explained on page 125.

If an employer issues a notice of dismissal which the employee regards as unfair, then an application can be made to an industrial tribunal at any time after the notice has been received and within three months of the termination date. Industrial tribunals hold fairly informal hearings and, as we have said, it is not necessary to be legally represented.

There are three possible results of a successful action for unfair dismissal: first the re-engagement of the employee (not necessarily in the same job or on the same terms); secondly the reinstatement of the employee (where he will be regarded as if he had not been dismissed); and thirdly compensation. The first two remedies involve the return to employment by the complainant, so the tribunal will always ask the employee whether he or she wishes to return to work. Obviously the tribunal will need to take this into account, in addition to the practicability of the employee returning to work with the former employer and indeed the strength of feeling on each side. Orders for re-engagement and reinstatement are rare. If no order is made for re-engagement or reinstatement, then the tribunal will award compensation which comprises a basic award based on length of service, pay, and age; and a compensatory award which will be a sum of money that the tribunal considers reasonable for the loss that the employee may have suffered due to dismissal. If the employer fails to comply with an order to re-engage or reinstate an employee, then the employee may get additional compensation.

## Redundancy

An employer must make a lump sum payment to anybody working for him who is dismissed because of 'redundancy'. Redundancy means a dismissal caused by an employer's need to reduce the work force. It may arise because a work place is closing down or because fewer workers are needed. In the ordinary course of events the employee's job must have disappeared. It will not be classified as redundancy if the employer engages a direct replacement as soon as the employee has been made redundant. In order to qualify for a redundancy payment the employee must generally have worked for at least two years for the employer for 16 hours a week or more; or for at least five years for 8 hours a week or more. Employment before the age of 18 does not count towards this qualifying period.

Redundancy payments are based on a calculation made on the basis of a week's pay and the number of years of service. If an employee is aged between 41 and 60 (for a woman) or 65 (for a man) the calculation is 1½ weeks pay for each complete year of employment. For those between the ages of 22 and 41 the calculation is one week's pay for each complete year of employment and for those aged between 18 and 22 half a week's pay for each complete year of employment. The maximum number of years service which may be counted for redundancy payments is 20. These are the statutory requirements for making somebody redundant, though many employers will in fact make larger payments at their own discretion.

Any person who is given notice of dismissal due to redundancy is entitled to be given a reasonable time off with pay during working hours by his employer to look for another job or to seek training courses. This again applies where the employee has had two years' continuous employment with the employer and works more than 16 hours a week, or where there has been 5 years continuous employment working between 8 and 16 hours a week. Again again certain people are not covered by this provision. They include the police and the armed forces; fishermen as described previously; registered dock workers engaged on dock work; and merchant seamen. Again the law does not specify what a reasonable amount of time for seeking alternative employment is, and it is inevitable that this will vary according to the circumstances of the particular employee and the number of interviews which he needs to attend. Anybody who is unreasonably refused time off for such purposes may complain to an industrial tribunal. If a successful complaint is made, then the tribunal will order the payment of the employee for the time taken to pursue interviews.

## Notice

One of the other things which have to be specified in your written contract of employment is a minimum period of notice to be given by either the employer or the employee. An employer has to give an employee at least one week's notice if he has been employed for more than one month but less than two years; at least two weeks notice after two years employment, and an additional week's notice for each complete year of employment for a period of less than 12 years; and at least 12 weeks notice if the employee has been employed for 12 years or more. An employee is required to give his employer at least one week's notice if he has been employed for one month or more. It is, however, open to anybody to contract for a longer notice period, and many salaried employees are on one, three, or even six months notice. The right to a minimum period of notice does not apply to civil servants and members of the armed services, registered dock workers engaged on dock work, merchant seamen on British ships of 80 gross tons or more, seamen on fishing boats; or to most employees who have fixed term contracts.

These then are some of the rights we all have in relation to our working environment. The law is very complex in employment matters and if you have a particular problem relating to work, we suggest that you contact your own trade union or the Department of Employment in your own area. We can do nothing more than outline some of your basic rights and each individual case has to be assessed on its merits.

# 8 Death

Everyone has the right to decide what should happen to the things which they own. This of course is true when you're alive, but it's perhaps more important on death.

## WILLS

During a lifetime, possessions will have been amassed and it is usual to want to make use of the right to say what should happen to them when you die and can no longer have a use for them. This is why people make wills. And what is a will? A will is a declaration of what you would like to happen to your property after your death. It is normally a formal written document and it can be changed at any time before your death, provided you are of sufficiently sound mind to do so and have not been forced into it.

A minor, in other words someone under the age of 18, cannot make a will – with the exception of a soldier, sailor or airman who is in actual military service at the time of making it.

The statute governing the making of a will is the Wills Act 1837. This sets out the formalities – for example that a will must be in writing signed by the maker (called the 'testator') in the presence of two or more witnesses. (A blind person cannot be a witness.) If the testator is very elderly or perhaps senile, it is often a good idea to include their doctor as a witness so that he can check that the person is capable of understanding the will and capable of making it.

The witness does not have to see the contents of the will, but must see the testator sign it or acknowledge it as his own. Because the purpose of a witness is to be an independent person, he cannot be a beneficiary under the will (otherwise he will lose any bequest). An attestation clause is no longer necessary.

The presumption is always that what is contained in the will are the wishes of the testator. Where ambiguities arise, it will become a matter for the courts to decide what the intentions of the testator were. It is to avoid such situations and their consequent expense that it is advisable to ask a solicitor to draw up your will for you. This is not an expensive exercise – you may be eligible for legal advice under the Green Form Scheme (which covers wills) and, failing that, most solicitors would not charge more than £20 unless the will is complicated. This will give you peace of mind, knowing that your wishes have been clearly expressed and that your property can be disposed of as you wish. Lawyers tend to make a lot of money from sorting out home-made wills which are uncertain and ambiguous. The Administration of Justice Act 1982 allows a court to order rectification of a will if it fails to carry out a testator's intentions because of a misunderstanding or a clerical error.

Before making a will it is sensible to draw up a list of all your possessions together with a list of the people you wish to benefit from your will. You should then work out who is to get what. Once the will has been drawn up it is important to keep it in a safe place. The will must name the personal representatives of the testator – the 'executors' – whose responsibility it is to carry out the wishes expressed in the will on your death. Unlike witnesses, executors are perfectly entitled to benefit from the will and indeed it is often a close relative who is appointed the executor of an estate. Only one executor is needed, but it's wise to appoint two in case one of them dies before you do.

It is important to make sure that the executors have been told where the will is kept, to enable them to begin the administration of the estate as soon as possible after your death.

## Revocation of a will

An existing will can be revoked at any time during the lifetime of the testator. The most common method is by making a new will which begins with the words 'I hereby revoke all former wills and codicils made by me' (a codicil is an addition to a will which is formally witnessed in the same way as a will). The deliberate destruction of a will does revoke it but the mere writing of the word 'revoked' across the face of the document is not enough to revoke it (unless the amendment is signed with witnesses present as if it was a new will).

A will is automatically revoked on the marriage of the testator. An exception is a will made before marriage which includes a sentence saying it is being made in contemplation of marriage to a specified person. It is therefore important when you marry, and perhaps even more important when you re-marry, to examine your will and make a new one.

Divorce will alter the validity only of gifts made to the divorced spouse. These will automatically become invalid on divorce but this does not alter the intentions expressed in any other part of the will. Again there may be an exception where a will is made in contemplation of divorce and where the testator, despite the divorce, still wants to leave part of his estate to his ex-spouse.

## If a person dies without a will

If there is no will then the estate passes to what are called the 'administrators'. The administrators are effectively the next-of-kin; if there are none the estate is dealt with by the Treasury Solicitor. Once it has been decided who is entitled to administer the estate, that person must apply to the Probate Registry for letters of administration – the court's confirmation of his appointment.

The duly appointed administrators of the estate will then have to distribute the belongings of the dead person according to the intestacy rules laid down in the Administration of Estates Act 1925 and the Intestates Estates Act 1952.

These rules may well not be exactly what you would have expected or wanted. The surviving spouse will receive all the 'personal chattels', including household possessions, clothes, cars etc. He or she will in addition receive a financial sum of £40,000. If there are any assets remaining, the spouse's further entitlement will depend on other relations. For example, if there are children, one half of the remainder of the estate will be held on trust for the rest of the spouse's life (giving him or her an entitlement to the interest earned by the sum held on trust).

If there are no children, but there are parents or brothers and sisters, the spouse will receive an additional £85,000 plus half the amount left over.

If there are no children, no grandchildren, no parents, and no brothers, sisters, nephews or nieces, then the surviving spouse will take everything.

## What are the children and grandchildren entitled to?

If there is a surviving spouse, then obviously the children will take half of what is left after the £40,000 and the personal possessions have been handed over. The other half goes to the surviving spouse for life and then to the children on the spouse's death.

If there is no surviving spouse then the children automatically inherit the whole estate equally.

If there are children, no other more distant relation will receive anything. If there is a surviving husband or wife but no children, the other relations will be entitled to the remaining half after the personal belongings and £85,000 have been distributed to that spouse. That half will go to the parents of the person who has died, in equal shares; or to the brothers and sisters (or their children if the parents are no longer alive).

If there is no surviving husband or wife, and no children of the person who has died, other relatives will inherit in the following order:

* parents
* brothers and sisters
* half brothers and half sisters
* grandparents
* uncles and aunts
* uncles and aunts of half blood

If there are none of these then the estate passes to the Crown.

A person who dies without leaving a will is known as an 'intestate': it is possible for someone to die partly intestate – if, for example, a bequest is made in a will to someone who dies before the testator. If this happens, then the part of the estate which would have gone to that person is divided up according to the intestacy rules above.

## Provisions for dependents

It is clearer today than it has been before that it is vital to make a will, particularly with the increasingly common incidence of split families and illegitimate births. During the twentieth century there has been an increasing awareness of the needs of people 'dependent' on a person's estate, and the current law governing this is the 1975 family provision legislation. This foresees three types of possible dependents who may not have been included in a will and who might normally expect to be entitled to continue to benefit from the income or estate of the testator. They are a surviving husband or wife; children of the dead person; and other dependents, whether or not they are members of the testator's family. (This may, for example, include a long-standing mistress.)

If such a person has not been provided for in the will then, if they can show that they were reasonably and wholly dependent on the dead person, they are entitled to apply to the High Court (or the county court if the estate is worth less than £30,000) for the will to be altered to make provision for them.

## Probate

When someone has died, their affairs have to be wound up, their possessions disposed of according to their wishes, and all financial matters closed. To enable an executor to do this he applies for a 'grant of probate', which is the formal certification by the Probate Registry that the executor is entitled to deal with the estate. The equivalent for administrators (where there is no will) is a grant of 'letters of administration'.

What needs to be done before probate is granted?

An application form, together with another form dealing with Capital Transfer Tax calculations, one dealing with any 'real property' (houses, flats or other land) and one dealing with stocks and shares must be filled in and sent to the registrar. Also to be sent are a copy of the death certificate and the will of the person who has died. If the estate is worth less than £40,000 there is no need for Capital Transfer Tax forms, and if the estate is very small then you may not need probate at all because some institutions will repay money they are holding if you simply send them the death certificate.

The person applying may have to attend an interview to satisfy the probate office that all debts etc. have been paid and all assets realised. It will also of course help to iron out any other difficulties which may have arisen.

After this, the application for the grant of probate is to be made. This involves more forms as well as the four already filled in: a Capital Transfer Tax form, a tax warrant with a copy of the will attached, a cheque for the relevant amount of Capital Transfer Tax payable to the Inland Revenue, and a cheque for the probate fee.

Some time later the executor will be sent the Grant of Probate and the estate can then be administered or disposed of. This will mean closing down bank accounts, building society accounts and the like; paying bills, collecting any tax refunds, payment for the funeral and so on.

When all this has been done, then the assets can be distributed in accordance with the terms of the will.

The administration of an estate is a time-consuming business and there are all sorts of snags and pitfalls which can arise if you have not made your wishes clear for the disposal of your assets.

This is one right which you can be certain will be enforced, so make sure there is a will to enable those you want to benefit to do so. Think particularly about the importance of exercising this right if you have been divorced, have children from more than one marriage, have adopted or foster children or have illegitimate children.

Your right is to dipose of your property and their right is to receive it as you would wish. Your duty is to make sure that happens.

# Bibliography

Page

7   Pritchard, John
    *The Penguin Guide to the Law*, Second Edition, Penguin,
    1985

9   Dicey, A.V.
    *Introduction to the Study of the Law of the Constitution*,
    Tenth Edition, Macmillan, 1959

10  Jennings, Sir Ivor
    *The Law and the Constitution*, Fifth Edition, University of
    London Press, 1959

14  Scarman, Lord
    *English Law – The New Dimension*, Stevens, 1974

17  Griffith, J.A.G.
    *The Politics of the Judiciary*, Third Edition, Fontana, 1985

17  Zander, Michael
    *A Bill of Rights?*, Third Edition, Sweet & Maxwell, 1985

19  Salmond, Sir John
    *Jurisprudence*, Twelfth Edition, Sweet & Maxwell, 1966

20  Hohfeld, Wesley Newcombe
    *Fundamental Legal Conceptions*, Yale, 1919

23  Hartley, T.C., and Griffith, J.A.G.
    *Government and Law*, Second Edition, Weidenfeld &
    Nicolson, 1981

33  Kellner, Peter, and Crowther-Hunt, Lord
    *The Civil Servants*, Macdonald, 1980

34  Lynn, Jonathan, and Jay, Anthony
    *Yes Minister*, Volume Three, BBC, 1983

34 Davies, Malcolm
*Politics of Pressure*, BBC, 1985

36 Denning, Lord
*The Discipline of Law*, Butterworths, 1979

37 Zander, Michael
*The Law-Making Process*, Weidenfeld & Nicolson, 1980

41 Jackson, R.M.
*Enforcing the Law*, Penguin, 1972

42 Fine, Bob, and Miller, Robert
*Policing the Miners' Strike*, Lawrence & Wishart, 1985

45 Baldwin, John
*Pre-Trial Justice*, Blackwell, 1985

56 Jackson, R.M.
*The Machinery of Justice in England*, Fifth Edition, Cambridge, 1967

57 Bagnall, Kenneth
*Judicial Review*, Profex, 1985

57 Aldous, Grahame, and Alder, John
*Applications for Judicial Review*, Butterworths, 1985

78 Devlin, Lord
*Trial by Jury*, Stevens, 1956

79 Ponting, Clive
*The Right to Know*, Sphere, 1985

85 Hargreaves, Fiona, and Levenson, Howard
*A Practitioner's Guide to the Police and Criminal Evidence Act 1984*, Legal Action Group, 1985

85 Zander, Michael
*The Police and Criminal Evidence Act 1984*, Sweet & Maxwell, 1985

102 Supperstone, Michael
*Brownlie's Law of Public Order and National Security*, Butterworths, 1981

# Index